TAUNTON'S

FAMILY HOME
IDEA BOOK

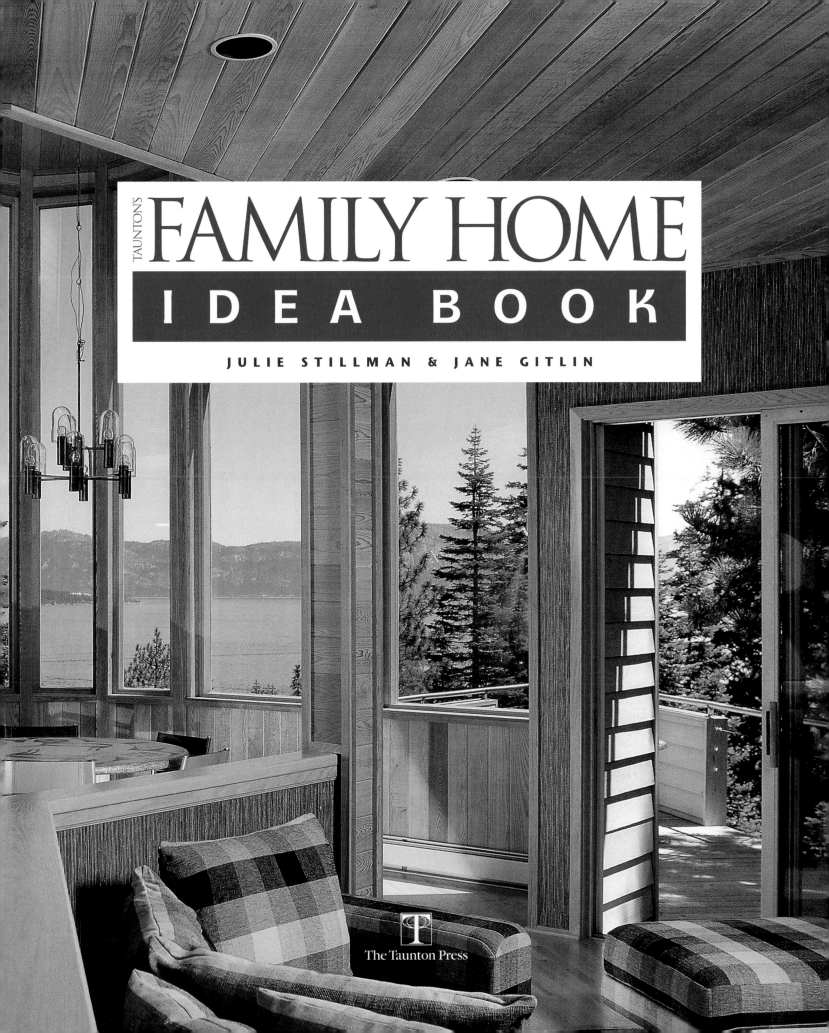

TAUNTON'S
FAMILY HOME
IDEA BOOK

JULIE STILLMAN & JANE GITLIN

The Taunton Press

To our families

The Taunton Press
Inspiration for hands-on living®

The Taunton Press, Inc., 63 South Main Street, PO Box 5506, Newtown, CT 06470-5506
e-mail: tp@taunton.com

Distributed by Publishers Group West

EDITOR: Stefanie Ramp
JACKET DESIGN: Cathy Cassidy
INTERIOR DESIGN: Lori Wendin
LAYOUT: Cathy Cassidy
ILLUSTRATOR: Christine Erikson
COVER PHOTOGRAPHERS: Front cover (top row, left to right): © Brian VandenBrink, Photographer 2003; © Jessie Walker; © Brian VandenBrink, Photographer 2003; (middle row, left to right): © davidduncanlivingston.com; Andrew Engel, courtesy Fine Homebuilding, © The Taunton Press, Inc.; © Brian VandenBrink, Photographer 2003; (bottom row, left to right): © Brian VandenBrink, Photographer 2003; © Rob Karosis; © Brian VandenBrink, Photographer 2003; (back cover, clockwise from top left): © Jessie Walker; © Jessie Walker; © Brian VandenBrink, Photographer 2003; © Jessie Walker;

Taunton's Family Home Idea Book was originally published
in hardcover in 2003 by The Taunton Press, Inc.

Library of Congress Cataloging-in-Publication Data
Stillman, Julie.
    Taunton's family home idea book / Julie Stillman & Jane Gitlin.
        p. cm.
    ISBN 1-56158-729-X (paperback)
    ISBN 1-56158-640-4 (hardcover)
    1. Architecture, Domestic--United States. 2. Room layout
(Dwellings)--United States. 3. Interior architecture--United States.
I. Title: Family home idea book. II. Gitlin, Jane. III. Title.
    NA7205.S74 2003
    728'.37--dc21
                        2003007727

Printed in the United States of America
10 9 8 7 6 5 4 3 2 1

Acknowledgements

Thanks to the Taunton family of editors, designers, and staff, who handle so many details so gracefully, with special thanks to Maria Taylor, Carolyn Mandarano, and Stefanie Ramp. Thank you to the many homeowners, designers, and builders whose homes are pictured here, and to the talented photographers who make each shot feel like home. Jane thanks Julie for being such a good correspondent, for being a talented writer, and for being so organized! Julie thanks Jane for her keen architectural insights, as well as her good humor while juggling the writing of several books, a full-time job, and a family.

Contents

Introduction

Home, sweet home. That may seem like an archaic saying from yesteryear, but on further reflection we realize it's a most contemporary expression of how we feel about the place we live. As our lives become increasingly frenzied—jam-packed with work, school, and serious play—we long to spend as much time at home as possible, "cocooning" with our families. And we want that home to be a haven for comfortable relaxation as well as a smooth-running machine.

The family home is no longer a series of formal rooms with rigid purposes, ruled by imperial parents. Today's home is a much more informal and versatile place than the one we grew up in, and certainly more kid-friendly (if not kid-obsessed).

Taunton's Family Home Idea Book was created to help you think about ways to design or renovate your home that speak to the needs of the whole family as well as its individual members. To assist in this

brainstorming exercise, we've put together hundreds of photographs that showcase practical and imaginative design ideas for comfortable living and family fun.

This book presents a realm of possibilities for family spaces. A home is made up of both public and private areas: The open floor plan that is so popular presents many opportunities for the family to mingle, but we also need separate territory where we can spend time alone.

The first section of this book focuses on the gathering places in the home, the primary areas where we congregate—living

In addition to the hundreds of photographs within these pages, there are numerous drawings and annotated floor plans that illustrate important concepts, such as making efficient use of existing space, establishing different zones within large spaces, and reviving outdated layouts. Sidebars throughout offer checklists for outfitting different family spaces, as well as suggestions for designing flexible spaces that adapt to the evolving needs of a family over time.

We hope this catalog of design ideas will inspire you as you make your house the home, sweet home you've always dreamed of.

rooms, kitchens, dining areas, and play spaces for kids of all ages. The next section turns to getaway places—the smaller, more private spaces, such as libraries and hobby rooms, or the private sanctuaries of bedrooms and bathrooms. This section also pays special attention to the nooks and crannies throughout the house that can be appropriated and reinvented as useful and appealing space. Of course, the outdoor "rooms" of the house make great family havens for open-air relaxation, so the last section of this book addresses porches, decks, patios, and outdoor play spaces.

The New Family Zone

I t is not a cliché to say that in the last few years we've become much more aware of how precious our time together is, and with our exceptionally busy lives, it's important that the physical space we inhabit is comfortable, convenient, and efficient for the way families live in the 21st century. We want our homes to be a reflection of who we are and how we interact with each other.

What constitutes a family has evolved in recent generations. While the traditional family unit still exists, families now are just as likely to be single-parent families, divorced parents sharing the kids, blended "Brady Bunch" families, empty-nesters or retirees, or multigenerational families. Today's homes

need to be flexible enough to accommodate this expanded definition of *family* and its evolving needs.

Society has changed as well, affecting the way we live and interact. Many people are self-employed and work from home, and telecommuting has become increasingly common, which calls for some sort of in-home workspace. Also in recent years, we've been bombarded by an array of new media equipment—for work and entertainment. Our living space must now accommodate home theaters, DVD, video games, CD burners, laptops, and scanners to name a few. Aside from just figuring out how to use all this newfangled equipment, we need to

◄ AN OPEN FLOOR PLAN ALLOWS FOR LONG VIEWS through the house to the outside, increasing the sense of space and the sense of attunement to the simultaneous activities going on in the house. In this house, different zones within the space are defined by columns, beams, and a low partition that separates the dining area from the seating area beyond.

make space for it in our homes without allowing it to overwhelm the place. And because parents and kids alike now have such complex schedules—packed with work, school, sports, and a million other activities—home life has become busier yet more casual. For instance, there just isn't time for a formal family meal every night.

So in a world where even playtime must be scheduled in advance, it's especially important that family leisure time be pure relaxation. It's essential to design the home for casual interaction, while still making it suitably elegant for guests and entertaining. The house needs to work for the immediate family for everyday living, but it also needs to gracefully accommodate the range of activities that brings others into our homes, from a cup of coffee with a neighbor to Thanksgiving dinner with family to a cocktail party for colleagues.

In looking at all these factors that push and pull on families today, there are several key elements to concentrate on when designing or remodeling a home. Above all, the design needs to focus on informal, comfortable gathering places, like the kitchen and living room, that encourage the family to spend time together. On the other hand, harmonious living depends on family members having some designated places within the home to retreat to, such as a bedroom or den, for private time, so the design should include getaway space as well. Another element to consider is how to make the best use of outdoor space, including outdoor "rooms" like porches, decks, and patios, and open space, such as the yard and driveway.

▲THIS 200-YEAR-OLD HOME was greatly altered to reflect the needs and desires of a 21st-century family while retaining the charm of its ancestor. Claustrophobic ceilings were blown out to create this two-story space for the dining area, where a built-in sideboard backs onto a built-in sofa, making efficient use of the space.

GATHERING PLACES

In our homes, we congregate for the communal activities of cooking, eating, playing, and hanging out. These pursuits can take place inside or outside the house, and we want versatile areas that are conducive to these activities—places that provide a cozy yet compelling backdrop for enjoying our time with others.

Living Informally: The Open Floor Plan

An open floor plan, which has particular zones for different uses instead of many smaller rooms with distinct purposes, is the key to gathering space in the modern home. The open floor plan offers a much more informal way of living, and in addition to encouraging the family to be together, this type of space can seem larger than its square footage might indicate. Most of today's open floor plans revolve around a "great" room: one large space that replaces formal living and dining rooms and often includes the kitchen as well. The zones in this big space

▲ THIS OPEN KITCHEN has several activity zones. A long peninsula work counter features an accessible sink at one end and an appliance garage at the other. In another zone, a built-in banquette forms a half-wall separating the eating area from the seating area beyond.

OPEN FLOOR PLAN

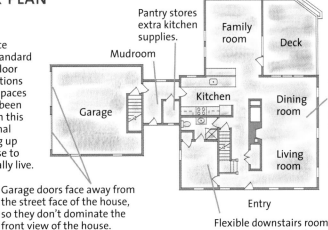

Although at first glance this appears to be a standard "center hall colonial" floor plan, the interior partitions that segregate living spaces from each other have been abolished. Homes with this same degree of informal planning are springing up everywhere in response to the way families actually live.

Pantry stores extra kitchen supplies.

Mudroom

Family room

Deck

Garage

Kitchen

Dining room

Living room

All meals take place at a friendly dining table adjacent to the deck, kitchen, and both living spaces (family room and living room).

Garage doors face away from the street face of the house, so they don't dominate the front view of the house.

Entry

Flexible downstairs room can be used as a bedroom, den, or kids' playroom.

▶ AS THE HUB of the family home, many kitchens have a dedicated area for a computer or small office. A pleasant spot like this in the kitchen is accessible to everyone; homework can be done within the cook's view, and it's a place to leave phone messages, check recipes and e-mail, or pay bills.

▼ DESIGNING A ROOM EXCLUSIVELY FOR PLAY is a modern notion of home planning. Here, a two-sided counter holds games and toys while dividing the room into two distinct play areas. Setting the pool table down a few steps keeps it from overwhelming the room with its size.

can be defined in any number of ways: by physical or built boundaries, by the arrangement of furnishings, or by unique focal points, such as a distinctive view or a fireplace. When planning the zones, it's also important to plan circulation paths, which should have an organic flow that directs movement and helps define the zones.

GETAWAY PLACES

There's something in all of us that wants our own personal sanctuary, the private place we can escape to for independent pursuits—studying, working, hobbies, sleeping. These rooms have a different set of requirements: perhaps a door to shut out the world, insulation from unwanted noise or extra electrical or communication lines. And private spots don't always have to be secluded; a well-placed window seat at the periphery of a gathering space can be a terrific getaway spot.

▲ FOR THE ARTISTICALLY INCLINED, the art studio is an essential getaway place, with no clocks or timetable to limit or measure creativity. Lighting is key for the painter—the track light fixtures here are an inexpensive and adaptable source of lighting, and a skylight brings in additional light. A rocking chair adds a homey touch—it can be used to relax and contemplate or to pose the model.

SEPARATING THE MASTER SUITE

In this plan, the master suite is separated from the main living area of the first floor. This creates a personal getaway for daytime activities or at night.

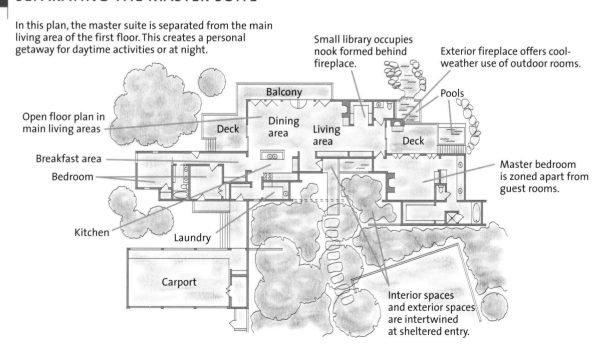

Small library occupies nook formed behind fireplace.

Exterior fireplace offers cool-weather use of outdoor rooms.

Pools

Balcony

Dining area

Living area

Deck

Open floor plan in main living areas

Deck

Master bedroom is zoned apart from guest rooms.

Breakfast area

Bedroom

Kitchen

Laundry

Carport

Interior spaces and exterior spaces are intertwined at sheltered entry.

Efficient Use of Space

Because getaway places tend to be smaller than our gathering places, using existing spaces to their full potential is a key planning consideration. With a little keen planning, for instance, some quirky space under the eaves can be liberated for an art studio, or a landing might make way for a small desk or library. So when planning getaway spaces in your home, don't think in terms of "rooms"; instead, think about activities and what they require, and then go on a hunt for bits of unused space that fit those requirements—you'll be surprised how much extra room you have. Once you've designated getaway space, outfit it with well-designed storage that's appropriate to the types of activities you'll be doing there.

▲IN THIS SLEEK AND MODERN SUITE, a pocket door rolls into the bookcase and divides the space into distinct zones so that when one person wants to read, the bed alcove can be closed off and the other can sleep or watch TV without being disturbed or disturbing. The same floor material flows from one area to the other, providing a unifying plane that links the two surfaces.

Often our getaway places must be shared space: bedrooms, closets, and bathrooms, for example. But even in shared bedrooms it's possible to create a retreat within a retreat—individual alcoves for each child, or a separate seating area within a master suite. Closets can be placed between adjoining bedrooms to create acoustic baffles; bathrooms can offer everyone his or her own sink and storage cubby.

USING SPACE EFFICIENTLY

Compact living space has long lines of sight, both across rooms and through changes in level. This enlarges the perceived space of a small home.

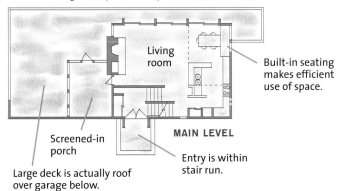

Living room

Built-in seating makes efficient use of space.

Screened-in porch

MAIN LEVEL

Large deck is actually roof over garage below.

Entry is within stair run.

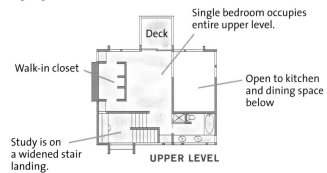

Single bedroom occupies entire upper level.

Deck

Walk-in closet

Open to kitchen and dining space below

Study is on a widened stair landing.

UPPER LEVEL

▲THE MUDROOM has become an essential room in the family home—a transition space between the public and private worlds. Deep wall niches here maximize storage potential with hanging rods, closed cabinets, benches, drawers, and low shelves. The checkerboard floor pattern solves the design problem of unifying the angled and straight sections of the hallway.

▲THIS EXTRA-DEEP WINDOW SEAT within a small bump-out off the living room makes a great escape. It offers an intimate getaway spot on the periphery of a large gathering space, offering distance from the hubbub while remaining open enough to retain a connection. Windows are on two of three sides, leaving one side for the reading lamp.

◄A BOOTH IS A COMFORTABLE and efficient dining space, perfect for casual breakfasts and lunches, and it's a very good use of space, particularly when space is at a premium.

►A CONNECTION TO NATURE in the form of an outdoor room offers a family a contained spot to gather. This pergola over a wooden deck shades the doors into the house and gives a place for vines to grow, linking the house with the natural landscape. A stone retaining wall marks the side of the cascading stairs leading to more outdoor rooms.

▼WHO NEEDS SLEEP-AWAY CAMP if this is your family's summer place? There are lots of options for enjoying the outdoors (and the family) here. The dock and a small cabin at the waterfront are where everyone wants to be on the nice days, and several porches at "the big house" are great for rainy-day or evening activities.

OUTDOOR SPACES

In this age of technology, our desire for a return to nature means more people are rediscovering and reconnecting to the open air. Hobbies like gardening, outdoor sports, birding, and other outside activities enjoy new popularity as healthy and available antidotes to the intensive work and school week. Of course, the yard is the ultimate play space for kids of all ages, so we are designing our homes to optimize our time outside by knitting the house into the landscape.

CONNECTING INDOOR AND OUTDOOR ROOMS

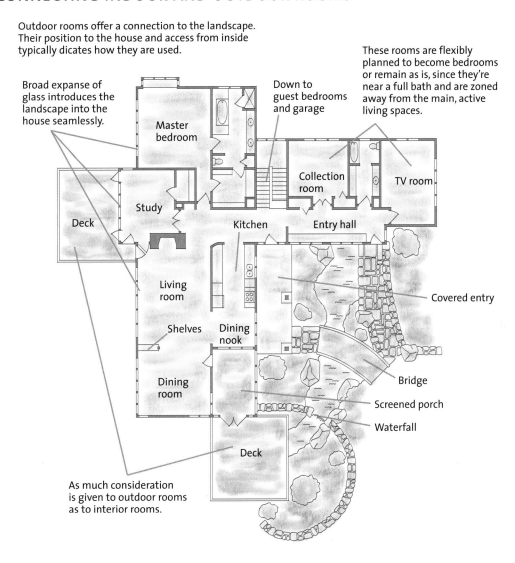

Outdoor rooms offer a connection to the landscape. Their position to the house and access from inside typically dicates how they are used.

Broad expanse of glass introduces the landscape into the house seamlessly.

Down to guest bedrooms and garage

These rooms are flexibly planned to become bedrooms or remain as is, since they're near a full bath and are zoned away from the main, active living spaces.

Master bedroom

Collection room

TV room

Study

Deck

Kitchen

Entry hall

Covered entry

Living room

Shelves

Dining nook

Bridge

Dining room

Screened porch

Waterfall

Deck

As much consideration is given to outdoor rooms as to interior rooms.

Some of our happiest family time is spent in those spaces between the living room and the yard—on the porch, deck, or patio. There we can relax in the great outdoors but still have the conveniences of an indoor room—the ability to cook, eat, and listen to music, for example. What makes these outdoor rooms most successful is the way they sit in the landscape and provide a sequence of movement from inside to outside—a gradual transition, either physically or visually, into an increasingly natural environment.

This might include moving through French doors onto a deck that looks out on a lawn with a view of the woods in the background.

FLEXIBLE FAMILY SPACES

Above all, we want our homes to be able to change as the family changes. Newlyweds give way to young families, then, unfortunately, perhaps divorced households, which entails kids being comfortable in two homes—always a juggling act. The family with teenagers is a different beast altogether,

▲EVEN AS NEW HOUSES ARE GETTING LARGER, we continue to exploit the spaces that we have in our older homes. This dreary basement was converted into an appealing living space—not the paneled rec room of your youth. The archway in the foreground helps hide the edge of a closet that encloses a water heater.

with a greater need for getaways (for both parents and kids). But time together can be especially important at this stage—having an inviting rec room to hang out in means that your teens can still be safely under your roof, but gain a sense of independence and privacy. Empty-nesters are able to reclaim the home for themselves, but it's still the center of family gatherings. For multigenerational families under one roof, some retooling may be needed to ensure that older members with physical limitations can still live comfortably in the home.

Flexible family space can be space that does double or triple duty—the guest room that's also the computer or hobby room. Or flexibility can come in the form of reinventing a space—the basement playroom that's converted to a family exercise room, and later morphs into a darkroom for the empty-nest photographer.

NEW FAMILY SPACES

As we spend more time than ever designing, furnishing, and tweaking our homes, we're developing a new level of sophistication. Sentimentality and nostalgia have a place, but the old notions are being challenged and expanded as fresh ideas are explored. New homes are being built in traditional styles—colonials, Capes, and bungalows—but designers are literally tearing down the walls of the past and replacing them with versatile open spaces that can accommodate and adapt to today's family.

In the pages that follow, you'll find a photo gallery containing hundreds of inspiring ideas for how our gathering, getaway, and outdoor spaces can work together to make a dynamic, comfortable, and beautiful family home.

REVIVING OUTDATED FLOOR PLANS: THE DINING ROOM REVISITED

TRADITIONAL ARRANGEMENT
Traditionally furnished dining rooms don't always see a lot of use, especially when another table is used in the kitchen or family room for most meals. Why not reconsider how to use that space?

YOUNG CHILDREN AT HOME
Relocating an infrequently used dining table to the large living room accomplishes two things: The former dining room can be used as a playroom for young children (close to the kitchen), and the shared eating/relaxing space becomes less formal—a good deal all around.

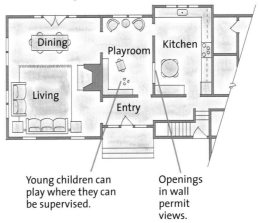

Young children can play where they can be supervised.

Openings in wall permit views.

EMPTY-NESTERS
Dining rooms can also be used as studies or libraries. Near a large social space, they are not soundproof, but are accessible for everyday desk work or an escape from the TV. Proximity to the kitchen is beneficial when multitasking.

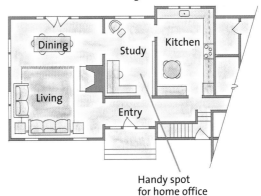

Handy spot for home office

Gathering Places

I N MORE FORMAL TIMES, our homes consisted of a number of separate rooms with specific functions: some designated exclusively for grown-ups, some exclusively for children, and some for more utilitarian use, like kitchens and bathrooms. Today, many new homes are designed with an open floor plan, using different zones to define the various functions of the space, and older homes are remodeled or adapted to gain the same informal, open spaces that encourage the mingling of lives. These are shared spaces where the whole family congregates to cook, eat, play, entertain, or just hang out together.

These gathering places—living spaces, kitchen and dining areas, and play spaces—are at the heart of family life; they are communal areas in which we can be with the family or get together with friends and relatives. As the setting for a wide range of activities and social occasions, it's essential that these spaces be thoughtfully designed to provide the comfortable havens we crave.

Gathering places can evolve over time, so it's important to consider how a room can be used for different purposes as the family's needs change. An unused dining room could become a toddler's playroom today, be converted to a teen hangout tomorrow, and be an empty nester's billiard room or study later.

◄ALTHOUGH THIS SPACE IS VERY LARGE, there are several distinct regions that offer an oasis of comfort within the larger space, inviting a tête-à-tête, a shared meal, or a convivial celebration. In the kitchen, a huge island offers seating for casual meals, while a cozy seating area with a fireplace and TV lies beyond. But the focal point is the dining area, defined by an octagonal rug that mirrors the spectacular octagonal trompe l'oeil ceiling.

Living Spaces

▲ THERE'S A SLEEK LOOK to this space with its dark trusses and columns that delineate the space for different uses. The mezzanine's railing is a modern detail—airplane cables stretched between the uprights seem transparent and lighten the visual weight of the upper regions.

VARIOUSLY CALLED THE LIVING ROOM, great room, or family room, this is the space—expansive or intimate—that invites everyone to congregate and get comfortable. How the living space is arranged is a mirror of family activities and may be defined architecturally (with framed openings, alcoves, and partitions, and by changes in ceiling height and flooring, for example) or by the furnishings. Seats may be grouped in one single-focus arrangement, or several smaller groupings may be used in larger rooms to reflect a number of activities within the same space. In either case, it's important that each seating area has a focal point, whether it's a window with a nice view, a TV, artwork, or a fireplace. Whatever the setup, flexibility is key, as the arrangement is likely to change every few years as the family does.

▲ WINDOWS ON MULTIPLE walls enliven a room, preventing the harsh shadows that are cast from a single light source. This bank of windows goes a step further, creating a nearly transparent wall. The long bench helps maintain a sense of intimacy and balances the openness of the windows.

◀ CAPTURING THE ESSENCE of the open floor plan, this space supports large gatherings, with plenty of room for moving around the furniture. The clerestory windows draw light in so the upper balcony space isn't dim and shadowy.

◄ THIS OPEN LIVING SPACE is framed by a portal that's topped by a transom of open squares of slender wood trim, offering a symmetrical view through the room to the fireplace. White painted bookshelves contrast the natural finish on the overhead beams, illustrating that not everything has to match. A round window next to the window seat adds visual interest in a room full of squares and rectangles.

Flexible Family Living Spaces

WITH OPEN FLOOR PLANS, the movable furnishings can be used to define the space as much as the architecture, which makes it easier for the rooms to adapt to the changing needs of a family as it grows up.

- Families with infants and young kids will want to arrange their space so the children are nearby. It's also important to childproof so that breakable and dangerous items are out of reach. Installing childproof cabinet latches, placing temporary gates, and protecting electrical outlets are the first priorities, but don't forget to give away potentially poisonous plants, relocate pet dishes, and remove flimsy furniture from areas that children will frequent.

- School-age kids can play independently, and it makes sense to have a space that can be closed off so that music, TV, and noise are confined to one space. Glass doors or interior windows offer a discreet way to keep an eye on things.

- Teens want a place to get away from adults, so using converted attic and basement space may offer a good solution. Consider adding an extra layer of sound barrier—like solid core doors and insulated interior walls and floors—to help limit noise in the rest of the house.

- Empty-nesters may relish a return to a less hectic time and choose to reclaim a formal, segregated dining area for a cozy den or romantic dinners for two.

- Families with grandparents under the same roof need special consideration. Three generations at home might be the impetus for adding a ground floor bedroom and a bathroom with sturdy grab bars and nonslip floors.

CREATING ACTIVITY ZONES

▲ IN A SPACE THIS LARGE, there can
be many activities going on simultaneously. This two-story great
room ringed with a mezzanine
walkway uses numerous rugs to
help define the distinct zones.

▶ A WALL OF DOORS (at left) folds
back to connect the living area
with the balcony in this sophisticated space, where stone walls and
mesquite floors use local materials
to their best advantage. Built-ins
negate the need for a lot of furnishings. The space between the
seating and dining areas can be
used as a play area and provides
room to circulate during parties.

The Long View

THE VIEWS WITHIN the house are as important as views to the outside, especially in a small house or apartment. Long views increase the connections between spaces and people, creating the illusion of more space, and the ability to see one room from another prevents a sense of isolation or claustrophobia.

When designing living spaces, it's important to consider setting up the room in a manner that achieves the longest views, which are usually along the diagonal. If you're lucky enough to have captivating views outside as well, windows that frame long vistas only enhance the illusion.

Long, diagonal views through an L-shaped space lengthen the dimensions visually, even in a small loft apartment like this. When the long view is directed toward a window or a featured architectural element, like these large concrete columns, the effect is even better.

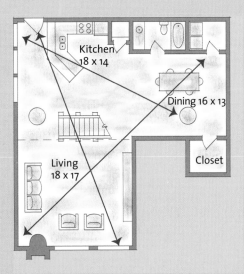

Kitchen
18 x 14

Dining 16 x 13

Closet

Living
18 x 17

◀ INTERESTING ARCHITECTURAL elements helped create this uncluttered living space that's conducive to entertaining. The planes of the ceiling are accentuated by the changing direction of the wood planks, and the ceiling material mirrors that of the floor, extending beyond the glass wall onto the roof overhang. With no solid walls separating the indoors from the outdoors, the space is connected to its surroundings and always blessed with beautiful views.

►THIS COLORFUL CURVED WALL reflects and accentuates the kitchen and makes a striking division between upstairs and downstairs. The space under a stairway can be the perfect place for storage and display if designed or modified thoughtfully.

▼COZY THROWS over the backs of the sofas mean snoozing is encouraged here. From the second-floor hallway you can see down to the family room and also across to the four-paned windows beyond. The barrel-vaulted ceiling brings the expanse down to a more domestic scale while preserving an open feeling. The niche on the left is custom-sized to hold a TV cabinet.

ESTABLISHING ACTIVITY ZONES

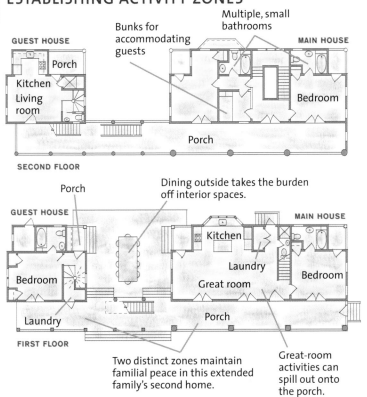

Bunks for accommodating guests

Multiple, small bathrooms

GUEST HOUSE

Porch

Kitchen

Living room

MAIN HOUSE

Bedroom

Porch

SECOND FLOOR

Porch

Dining outside takes the burden off interior spaces.

GUEST HOUSE

Bedroom

Laundry

FIRST FLOOR

MAIN HOUSE

Kitchen

Laundry

Great room

Bedroom

Porch

Two distinct zones maintain familial peace in this extended family's second home.

Great-room activities can spill out onto the porch.

▲ ONE LARGE ROOM that shares space for three activities—cooking, eating, and lounging—makes sense in a vacation house that accommodates many family members. This is Florida, so cool and shady interiors are a welcome contrast to the strong sun outside. The double-faced upper cabinets are accessible from both sides and permit light from the windows to shine in.

◄ THIS FAMILY WANTED their new home to feature aspects of colonial design, but with an open floor plan that is well suited to a modern family. The oversize 12-over-12 windows bring in plenty of light, and the 9-ft. ceiling contributes to the spacious feel.

▲ A ROOM LIKE THIS, which features a strong geometric shape, creates a focal point within a house, drawing family members in to recharge or to relax. The octagonal ceiling forms a protective shell around the living room, making it cozy but not claustrophobic.

◄ THE CEILING IS THE PRIMARY FOCUS in this room, giving it character and scale with exposed beams that envelop a windowed loft and making it the perfect playroom (out of the way but within earshot). At floor level, the rug anchors and defines the seating areas.

◄ THE HOMEOWNERS wanted a year-round retirement house on the same site as their summer camp. A two-story barn was built to accommodate both personal pursuits and large family gatherings; the first floor is used for boatbuilding and storage, while the second floor is used as the social center of the house for family reunions and as a year-round refuge for the retirees.

▼ AS IN THE HULL of an overturned boat, the spaces within this house are small and intimate. The bedroom, bathroom, and kitchen fit in two bays of the four-bay timber-frame barn, leaving the other half wide open for living and entertaining. Sufficient lighting is critical in a wood-paneled room, and the light coming in from the gable-end windows and the roof-ridge monitor window provide abundant natural light.

SEATING AREAS

▲THE POST-AND-BEAM STRUCTURE of the original home remains intact and serves as the bones of this current incarnation, which features a wall of French doors that open the room up to a panoramic vista outside. The long view through the house is accentuated by the rhythm of the overhead beams.

►A ROOM CAN HAVE multiple focal points as long as they don't compete; the aquarium and artwork here create a harmonious backdrop for the seating area, which focuses on both.

►USING LIGHTING LEVELS that can be changed or adjusted adds an energetic design element. Clearly, this is the home of an art collector, with carefully considered lights at the soffit aimed to shine on the painting over the fireplace and on the books. Standing lamps offer a more intimate supplement to overhead lighting, and placing them in multiple locations prevents harsh shadows.

◄INVENTIVE SHAPES and out-of-the-ordinary color combinations make this a fanciful family space. The architect/owner crafted these couches to be pulled apart into separate chairs—these pieces also feature star cutouts, storage within the backs, and unique, attached "end tables."

◄NOT ALL HOMES have great rooms. In this modest but intimate space, the dining area is punctuated and defined by the chandelier, and the seating area beyond is marked by an exposed beam. Plentiful windows make this room come alive and feel spacious.

▼THIS SEATING AREA is inviting because it's in the middle of the activity zone. The columns serve a number of purposes—they add a bit of architectural pizzazz, frame the seating area, and signal the change in floor levels.

◄THIS SPACE IS CAPTIVATING from top to bottom, starting with the unique framing at ceiling level. A quirky roofline mandated that the framing follow the same unusual slope and angles, and rather than cover it up inside, the architect chose to celebrate these structural gymnastics. The windows at the second level suggest a tree house, and the kids can have fun watching the grown-ups below. Having the stairs bring you directly into the seating area is a friendlier approach than stairs that drop you into a distant hallway.

◄A STRONG GRID PATTERN carries the design theme throughout this sunken living room, where the fireplace level is the focus of the seating area, with a step down into the "conversation pit." The backs of the couches don't block the view, and multiple skylights above the fireplace highlight the face of the stonework.

◀ MULTIPLE LEVELS make for visually interesting space and provide multiple zones for activities. Here, the levels imitate a theatre, with the center of activity "on stage," while cascading adobe walls embrace the view and the seating, and the two stairways enable a grand entrance or a quick exit. This is a great example of using traditional materials in a nontraditional way.

▼ DESIGNED TO TAKE FULL ADVANTAGE of the superb view, this living space has several seating areas. One (at right) is formed by a low partition where the high back adds a sense of security, and in the kitchen, stools are positioned for a view out the window. A higher ceiling above the round table signifies more activity in that area, and allows for taller windows to take in the view.

Partitions

PARTITIONS ARE USED TO MARK the edges of rooms and other zones within living spaces and can be fixed or flexible. Partitions can take the form of walls, half-walls, screens, glass panels, a bank of doors, fireplaces, or storage units. Low partitions are appealing because they can distinguish the space without cutting off views, giving the sense of one larger space. Higher, more solid partitions provide more privacy and better acoustic separation between spaces. Partitions, whether they are high or low, can also signal an appropriate place to change floor or wall finishes—going from wood to stone, for example.

▲ THERE ARE TWO DISTINCT ZONES in this living space, which is divided by a fat partition that incorporates the fireplace and two display platforms. Being able to see across the top of a fireplace is uncommon; here it is accomplished by using a slender metal flue instead of a traditional brick chimney. The zones are linked by a common ceiling height and by a distinctive mottled concrete floor.

▲THE INTERIOR SURFACES in this space are both finished and rustic, creating a room with a sense of comfortable modernity, while suggesting the accumulation of much time spent in this quaint country home. Keeping the house's original wide-plank floors amplifies this effect.

▶DOUBLE-HEIGHT SPACES can feel hollow. So trusses, beams, and other elements that pass through the high volume help define the space, giving it reference points and scale. There are several seating areas in this space—lots of couch space, and more intimate seating near the fireplace.

FIREPLACES

▶ THIS MASSIVE STONE FIREPLACE has real presence even when no fire is burning. Forgoing a conventional chimney that encases a flue, triple flues are exposed here, extending up in front of the window and creating a smokestack effect.

▲ THERE'S ENOUGH ROOM for three generations to gather in front of this substantial fireplace. The lines of horizontal timbers continue around the room, forming a band that distinguishes the walls, and the exposed structural frame adds a traditional character to this double-height space.

◀ A SPECIAL RECESS for the fireplace (called an inglenook) featuring a cozy bench was popular in Arts and Crafts homes and is reinterpreted here. Similarly, the tapered columns are a modern version of Arts and Crafts detailing.

▶THE UNDULATING WALL surface that forms this southwestern-style fireplace bracketed by window seats, creates a cozier feel than a flat, angular design would. Suggesting an organic shape, it gives the impression of a warm embrace around the fire.

▼AS THE FOCAL POINT of this warm but spacious space, the fireplace sits beneath a virtual canopy of naturally finished beams, which define the seating areas and tie the ceiling plane in to the built-in storage cabinets on the left. The long counter, positioned at table height, encourages collections and deposits of interesting artifacts.

THE HEARTH OF THE HOME

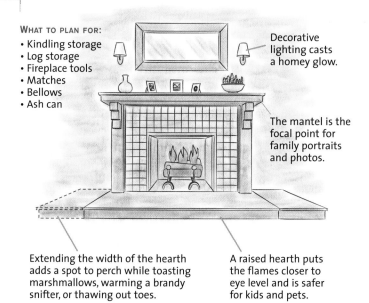

WHAT TO PLAN FOR:
• Kindling storage
• Log storage
• Fireplace tools
• Matches
• Bellows
• Ash can

Decorative lighting casts a homey glow.

The mantel is the focal point for family portraits and photos.

Extending the width of the hearth adds a spot to perch while toasting marshmallows, warming a brandy snifter, or thawing out toes.

A raised hearth puts the flames closer to eye level and is safer for kids and pets.

COLLECTIONS AND DISPLAYS

▶SUBSTANTIAL BUILT-IN shelves that form part of the architecture tend to have more aesthetic appeal than towering bookcase units that are plopped in a corner. Tucking storage and display space under a stairwell is a clever way to mine additional space from small rooms; even shelves that are shallow (such as the depth of a stud wall) are useful for showing off family treasures.

▼SPECIAL COLLECTIONS deserve a distinctive space to be enjoyed by all. Built-in shelving that runs up to the ceiling is perfect for display, and placing a seating area right in the heart of the space inspires fond memories and conversation.

◀REFLECTING THE HEART and soul of a family, the objects and memorabilia collected over the years are important to family life and should have some designated space. Displays will look less haphazard and cluttered if you plan this space, remembering that collections will evolve over the years. One way to do this is to build a wider wall to accommodate display nooks, as this family did.

Storing Our Toys

Families accumulate lots of playthings in their living spaces, and especially in a house with an open floor plan, it's important to reduce the visual clutter as well as have dedicated storage for complete cleanup when the space is being used for another purpose (such as entertaining).

So when planning your living area, make a list of all the items that need storage space—books, stereo, CDs, videoes, DVDs, games, photo albums, collections, sports equipment, and kids' toys. Then decide what's best for your needs—freestanding or built-in shelves, drawers, cabinets, or closets. The most effective storage generally includes open and closed options: A collection of books looks good on open shelving, while an army of action figures would do best behind closed doors.

▲NAUTICAL INSIDE AND OUT, this living room has enough cushy chairs for the whole family to read or nap on, and the angled walls take in the harbor view. Reflecting a passion for the wayfaring life and the house's location on the water, this living space show-cases boat models throughout the room.

▶BUNCHING UP all the storage where you can use it as a major design and display element is a splendid and practical idea. With so much storage in one place you don't have to search all the closets for one item that could be any-where. For easy reference, make a "map" of what's in each drawer.

Kitchens Plus

THE KITCHEN IS THE CENTER OF THE FAMILY UNIVERSE. From the smell of coffee brewing in the morning to the late-night bowl of ice cream, this room inexorably draws us in. Whether we convene there for a leisurely family meal or simply grab a slice of pizza on the way to Little League, the kitchen is the place we want to be—to linger, to loiter, to live in.

An open floor plan generally hinges on the kitchen, and this all-important room needs to be designed in a way that serves the many functions we require of it: a place to prepare and serve food, do home-work, pay the bills, entertain, feed the cat. You want to connect the kitchen, dining, and living areas comfortably, but also establish sepa-rate zones for distinct activities. Remember that good circulation paths in and around the kitchen are vital—you don't want a table or island to close off a prime pathway.

◄ COOKING IS A FAMILY ACTIVITY, as well as one that is shared with guests, and this fabulous kitchen was obviously designed for a family that likes to cook for a crowd. Pots and pans are within easy reach, and the wood-fired pizza oven and fireplace ensure that everyone will flock to the hearth, guaranteeing that the kitchen is truly the heart of the home.

Cooking with Kids

IT'S FUN FOR THE FAMILY to cook together, and it teaches kids to follow a recipe, measure accurately, and use appliances—eventually they'll be able to make those pancakes themselves and serve you breakfast! Here are some useful equipment suggestions to make cooking an enjoyable and safe experience for all:

• A sturdy pull-out step stool so kids can reach the work surface
• Low drawers for kid-sized access
• Oversized knobs on cabinets and drawers, which make it easier for kids to open them (works for older hands too!)
• Easily cleanable surfaces (stone or natural wood counters look great, but will acquire a patina of wear over time)
• A microwave placed on a lower shelf (a safe appliance for kids to use)
• A "kid's tools" drawer containing utensils that aren't too sharp but still let kids have a sense of ownership in the kitchen

▲ AS THIS MULTIFACETED space proves, the new family kitchen incorporates elements previously reserved for other rooms. Wood floors and fine carpets make their way into this space, and a comfortable wicker chair sets off a small seating area with a view. The raised ceiling above the French door has a skylight—a good way to get light into a room that often has its walls taken up with storage.

EAT-IN KITCHENS

▼A SIMPLE, PARED-DOWN peninsula divides this informal room, which makes effective use of inexpensive materials to create the ultimate family space: kitchen and playroom all in one.

▲A LARGE KITCHEN with many work surfaces and a pantry provides plenty of room for different family members to help prepare part of a meal for a big occasion. This island is in the center of a sea of kitchen components, including a restaurant refrigerator.

►A CORNERSTONE of the open floor plan, the clever use of multiple floor levels defines the boundaries of sub-spaces without resorting to walls. This well-thought-out space has a clear circulation path along the storage wall that doesn't interfere with any of the three family activity areas.

▶THREE IS *NOT* A CROWD at this island eating space, where the beadboard side panels of the island form a recess for the stools. Standard counter height is 36 in., so stools should measure accordingly.

▼THIS HOMEY KITCHEN has a counter height designed for each member of the family, which allows everyone to get into the act of cooking. The deep overhang at the wooden chopping block allows you to scoop items right into a bowl or pan—quite handy. The island not only provides extra counter and workspace, it's also a compelling visual focus for the room with built-up baseboard moulding details like that of fine furniture.

◄▼A LARGE MAPLE-TOPPED ISLAND anchors the plan for this kitchen, providing a large workspace as well as an informal dining spot. A variety of materials— from steel to wood to aspen branches (legs of island, side of baskets, shelves at sink)—enliven the room, and windows over both the sink and the stove keep things light. The kitchen is open to the dining room (see the floor plan) and features a fireplace with a small seating area and a porch that has been converted to a pantry.

AN OPEN FLOOR PLAN

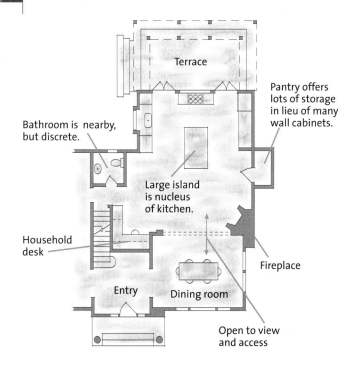

Terrace

Pantry offers lots of storage in lieu of many wall cabinets.

Bathroom is nearby, but discrete.

Large island is nucleus of kitchen.

Household desk

Fireplace

Entry

Dining room

Open to view and access

▲INTERESTING ANGLES at multiple levels give this kitchen a dynamic quality. Breakfast at the dining counter puts you at the center of family activity. One of the drawbacks of an open kitchen can be cooking odors. Here, an overhead vent at the range exhausts cooking steam and fumes.

▲THAT'S NO ISLAND, that's a continent—with six stools to accommodate the whole family. This particularly large island provides all the counter space in the kitchen, with storage on the ends and even a place to hang dishtowels. The raised section in the middle has electrical outlets, and it also shields the back of the stovetop and the sink. It's a simple layout, but one that is both effective and efficient.

►THERE IS A SCULPTURAL quality to the island in this curvaceous kitchen. The curves imply motion around the island, and the curve theme is echoed throughout the house. The island's central location within the open floor plan makes it *the* place to be during a party.

▶ THIS COMPACT KITCHEN is well designed and has a comfortable look and feel. A two-pronged countertop is made up of a bead-board base and a lower section that is a kitchen table. The table can be used to roll out dough (always easier at a lower counter), and the children can reach it if they want to get involved. The peekaboo cutouts in the upper wall give a glimpse of the ceiling and beams beyond, connecting the kitchen to the rest of the house.

◀ SEATING ARRANGED on two adjacent sides of an island permits diners to see one another—making it more like a table than a diner counter. This kitchen is built for entertaining, with two ovens, which allow the luxury of baking two things at once—a real timesaver.

▲ INEXPENSIVE PLASTIC laminate counters are very practical for family use—and they can be changed easily and economically if they get scorched or chipped. Plastic laminate is available in an enormous variety of colors and patterns but sometimes a simple white counter is best—it doesn't compete for attention if you want to use bright colors in other areas or put a lot of objects on display.

▶ THIS LARGE KITCHEN has two islands: one for food prep, the other for eating. The refrigerator is situated so that you can grab a drink without going through the cooking space, which a busy hostess will definitely appreciate. The contrasting white and dark-stained cabinets lend a tailored look that won't feel dated in a year or two.

◀A BUILT-IN BREAKFAST NOOK **is a** perfect spot for Sunday brunch or for laying out bills or homework. The floor material changes just before the top of the first descending riser, which helps signal the change in floor level (and is a subtle reminder not to move your chair back too far).

Flexible Family Kitchens

At DIFFERENT TIMES in your family's life cycle, there will be specific issues to consider in your kitchen setup. Keep the following points in mind when making initial design plans so your kitchen can flex with your family as needed.

- **Families with young children.** Safety concerns come first in a room filled with appliances that cut, grind, and burn. Stock a cupboard or drawer with playthings—including kitchen items like pots and pans—that will occupy the kids while a meal is being prepared. Plan the circulation through the kitchen so that kids aren't running underfoot as you drain pasta into the colander. Islands help create good circulation—one side is the business side, the other is for hanging out or walking past.

- **Families with older children.** Teach older kids how to use appliances and utensils so they feel comfortable cooking on their own. Locate the microwave in a spot where they can reach it without climbing on a counter.

- **Older couples.** Ergonomics are important for getting things done with ease in the kitchen. Use big knobs with texture on appliances and cabinets for arthritic hands to grab. Have plenty of light, natural and otherwise. Wall cabinets should be mounted lower, or use a pantry in lieu of wall cabinets. Dishwashers or wall ovens can be mounted higher than usual within a custom cabinet to ease all that bending over. Avoid uneven handmade floor tiles.

▲A DINING SPOT in the kitchen can be strictly utilitarian, or it can be designed to unify the architecture and the furnishings in elegant fashion. This table was designed as part of the architecture, with details similar to the window screening, and a wraparound built-in bench allows additional chairs to be pulled up. The refrigerator is situated close by for easy refills.

◄THIS INTIMATE BREAKFAST nook, with a built-in bench and loose chairs, is close to the kitchen counters to promote family time or provide a spot where guests can visit the cook. When planning built-in seating, allow room for the gentle slope at the back of the bench.

Kitchen Safety Checklist

SOME KEY CONSIDERATIONS for safety in the family kitchen:

- Locks on cabinets that contain dangerous equipment or toxic materials; these can be permanent or temporary gadgets.
- Enough electrical outlets—building codes require one every couple of feet at a counter and also at islands to avoid misuse of extension cords or cords being dragged across hot stove burners.
- A place to set hot pots when they come off the stove.
- Nonslippery flooring. Avoid little rugs that can trip you up.

▲BANQUETTES REDUCE THE AMOUNT of floor space required—no one has to move behind seated diners, and there's no need to allow clearance for chairs to pull out. This round niche has a drop-leaf table that can be enlarged for guests but saves space when not needed. The opening to the alcove is defined by the dropped beam and the stepped-down wainscot.

BOOTH REQUIREMENTS

Windows make a booth feel more spacious.

A depth of 24 in. to 30 in. seats one; 42 in. to 54 in. seats two; 60 in. to 74 in. seats three.

8° to 10°

36 in. to 48 in.

18 in.

30 in.

18 in.

24 in. minimum

18 in.

30 in. per seat, 24 in. minimum

3-ft. clearance minimum, 5 ft. preferred

◄BOOTHS MAKE A GREAT design solution when space is at a premium, and they are especially good for smaller homes because you can put a booth in a space as narrow as 5 ft. wide. This intimate space is set just apart from the action in the rest of the kitchen, so it doesn't interfere with food preparation.

▲JUST LIKE AT YOUR FAVORITE DINER, in this kitchen you can pull a stool up to the counter or snuggle in a booth. The step up to the nook brings the table up to the height of the windowsill, giving the sense that the table is on grade with the landscape outside, while natural tree trunks rise up through the room, creating the playful evocation of a tree house.

▶THIS ELEGANT BOOTH boasts a slab of granite and is fastened in place on two sturdy legs. Like a proscenium arch, the beam and posts at the front of the booth define and frame it, putting the diners into a family tableau. Natural light is an important consideration for eating areas, even if the views aren't picturesque, and windows placed on all sides of the booth keep it from getting claustrophobic.

◀IN THIS THREE-SIDED BOOTH, the bench is integrated into the side of the cabinets. Benches without cushions have to be carefully detailed and dimensioned, so that they are comfortable to lean back in and the knees aren't pinched under the table. Allow 30 in. along the length of the table for each diner to be comfortable. The freestanding trestle table could be replaced if the family wants a new look later on.

ISLANDS

▶ISLANDS COME IN MANY shapes and sizes, and this unusual one has multiple heights and surface materials. The drumlike portion has a butcher-block top for chopping and curved drawers for storage. A small but elegant granite serving area is attached, which could also double as a lower work area for little helpers.

◀IN THIS KITCHEN, the rectangular island is the main scullery station with a double sink and adjacent dishwasher incorporated, making it a convenient dish drop-off in relation to the dining table. The peninsula (foreground) hosts the stovetop and additional prep space. The islands' shiny counters are a strong contrast against the rough-hewn beams overhead.

▶FRIDAY NIGHT IS PIZZA NIGHT, but in this home that means more than calling for takeout. This "pizza island" was designed to get the whole family into the act of pizza making. Drawers and doors for trays and other equipment on both sides mean two chefs can make different pizzas simultaneously. The island is topped with a butcher-block top for rolling out the dough. Cleanup is easy with a slot that empties into a removable compost tray—complete with trash can underneath.

◀COOKING BECOMES a cooperative and communal family activity with this multipurpose island that has a cooktop, oven, storage space, and eating area all in one. It has two levels—one for cooking, one for eating. The unique chevron-shaped upper portion of the counter shields the stovetop from the diners' view.

Types of Islands

IN MANY HOMES, especially new ones, the kitchen island has taken on the multifaceted roles that the kitchen table served for years—a food preparation area, an informal eating spot, a large surface for homework and projects. Your cooking habits and the layout of your current kitchen will dictate what kind of island (if any) will add to the efficiency and convenience of your kitchen. Regardless, adding storage and outlets to any island will increase its usefulness.

Islands come in all shapes and sizes, but they generally come in the following configurations, equipped to serve numerous functions:

- Islands that simply provide a large counter surface are used solely for food preparation
- Islands that include a cooktop become a primary or secondary space for prep and cooking (it's especially useful to have two stoves if you cook or entertain a lot)
- Islands that include a cleanup sink and dishwasher and become the primary or secondary wash station (it's especially useful to have two sinks and dishwashers if you entertain a lot)
- Islands designed to accommodate seating on one or both sides, which can be used as an informal eating area, in addition to a work station

▲THIS ISLAND IS ALL BUSINESS— no knee space for stools here. The prep sink separates the cleanup area from the cooking area and closed storage on all sides keeps things looking sleek. Stainless-steel refrigerators repel magnets, so photos, report cards, and invitations need to go elsewhere.

◀THIS HARDWORKING ISLAND, with an end-grain chopping block and lots of storage for knives, features a microwave oven framed by a cabinet door that's been drilled with holes for ventilation. Putting the microwave down low makes it easy for the kids to use it.

THE KITCHEN AS A FAMILY HUB

◄ AS THE HUB OF FAMILY ACTIVITY, the kitchen is the hardest-working room in the house, and it pays to consider how areas can serve double duty. Here, a cozy breakfast nook is used for eating as well as making cakes and decorations for special occasions. It would serve equally well as a desk, with a phone close at hand and paperwork stowed in the nearby hutch.

▲ A KIDS' CORNER is a great way to keep little ones occupied in their own special spot, where they are under one's eye but not underfoot. A built-in desk keeps art supplies nearby. This space can be adapted later for other uses—more storage, the dog's bed, or the recycling bin.

▲ AN ADJUSTABLE-HEIGHT STOOL SWIVELS between the counter-height desk and the table-height extension of the island. The lower part of the island is good for rolling out dough, and it doubles as an eating area. The desktop can also be used as a bar or buffet when entertaining.

▲▶ THE COLORFULLY PAINTED chairs and table express the personalities of the people who sit on them in this creative kitchen full of homemade décor. In addition to the counter and table, this kitchen also has a desk/message center and a cookbook library. The stone countertop on the island overhangs at least 12 in. on the seating side—the minimum for comfort.

◀EVEN A LITTLE ANGLED COUNTER tucked into an out-of-the-way corner is better than no place at all to check your calendar. Having space for such objects, even if it's minimal, keeps the kitchen table from turning into a desk covered in clutter and papers.

Message Center Checklist

THE MESSAGE CENTER is a critical part of the family kitchen; it's the place where mail is sorted, phone messages retrieved, schedules posted, and family calendars consulted. Locate yours in an area that you have to pass by when leaving or entering the house. That way, it will be the natural spot to drop your bag or briefcase, the mail, and your car keys.

The ideal message center should have:

- some dedicated counter or desk space
- multiple outlets for the phone, answering machine, electric pencil sharpener, computer, lamp, clock
- a calendar
- phonebooks
- a bulletin board
- a chalkboard or other erasable board
- pigeonholes or cubbies for each family member
- a trash can for the junk mail
- junk drawer for tape, rubber bands, and other family flotsam and jetsom

▲THIS FAMILY'S COMMUNICATION CENTER is a French door that was reglazed with panes of porcelainized steel covered in a chalkboard finish. Each pane has a purpose—for to-do lists, shopping lists, messages, schedules, even artwork. There is space for everyone to leave messages or decorate the door.

◀IN THIS PHONE MESSAGE CENTER, the sloped counter has a lip to prevent papers from sliding off and a special cubby below for phonebooks. Above the counter, pigeonholes of varying sizes organize the mail and other items.

▶THE MESSAGE CENTER is an indispensable place in any family home. Too often, well-meaning folks plant it in a shielded, out-of-the-way location, but find that it doesn't "take." Putting the message center in a logical place along the path you automatically take when entering the house makes it far more likely that it will be used. The message center doesn't have to look makeshift or rickety; you can seamlessly incorporate it by purchasing components that match the kitchen cabinets.

►IN THIS KITCHEN, the message center is combined with a space-saving idea for a breakfast table or tea for two. Cookbooks are handy for menu planning, and the TV in the corner is good for catching the morning/evening news or keeping the kids occupied while dinner's cooking.

Setting Up the Family Kitchen

- In many new homes, there's a tendency to build much larger kitchens; this can be a boon if you spend a lot of time there, but not if the work area gets spread out in the process. When this happens, the kitchen's efficiency is diminished, as you're constantly trotting back and forth between different areas. Well-designed kitchens are measured by convenience rather than square footage.

- The notion of a rigid "kitchen triangle" is challenged every day and is somewhat obsolete. There is no single geometric formula that will work for every kitchen, so design your kitchen for your particular needs and work preferences.

- Plan for multiple zones—prep, cooking, and cleanup are three different procedures, and each requires different equipment. Assembling ingredients and chopping vegetables requires access to the fridge and pantry, as well as plenty of counter space. When cooking, you need to reach spices, pans, and utensils while keeping a close eye on what's simmering on the stove. Cleanup is easiest in a scullery arrangement with a dedicated deep sink and dishwasher out of the cook's way. With multiple zones, every family member can get into the act without stepping on each other's toes.

- Set up by your kitchen according to your routine. For example, put the coffeemaker next to the cereal cabinet, and both near the toaster and the breakfast table.

- Lighting is key—a flexible combination of adequate ambient and task lighting will work for cleaning, cooking, eating, or entertaining. Choose from fluorescent, incandescent, or low-voltage lighting, and add dimmers when possible for discrete lighting or romantic midnight suppers.

- Organize your storage. The everyday things need to be most accessible—basic pots and pans, everyday dishes, silverware, lunchboxes, leftover containers. Seasonal and special-occasion items—the punch bowl, the holiday dishes, the lobster pot—can be on the periphery or even in another room. Also, match the storage to the object—a deep drawer filled with tangled cooking tools will cause massive headaches; a couple of shallow drawers is a better alternative.

▼THIS HIGHLY FUNCTIONAL message center revolves around a cabinet door that's fitted with cork for a bulletin board. Below are cubbies for mail and drawers for all the important information that collects in a home (such as appliance warranties).

▲THIS CURVY CUSTOM DESK, located alongside the pantry, proves that a workstation doesn't have to be dull or purely practical. The desktop is the perfect size for a phone, TV, and writing area, and it could even accommodate a laptop computer. The drawers create generous closed storage for all the other paraphernalia that migrates to the family hub.

◄THIS UNUSUAL BUT HANDY station marries message center and wine cooler. The cork backdrop offers a home for everything from grocery lists to kid art, while the cubby drawers above organize paper clips, rubber bands, and the like far more effectively than one big drawer. During parties, the countertop can be pressed into service as a decanting station.

◀COMPUTERS NEED A SURPRISING amount of space, with printers, scanners, and other accessory hardware, and this kitchen devotes a corner to a mini-office. Most cabinet manufacturers are now making units that accommodate computers and other office needs and coordinate with the kitchen cabinets, as is the case here.

▼IN THIS NOOK, the breakfast bar converts to a mail center when the cabinet doors are retracted. Pigeon-holes make a handy spot for take-out menus and school schedules. The TV pulls out to keep the cook company or amuse fidgety kids waiting for dinner.

THE SMALL KITCHEN

▶MANY FAMILIES don't have the luxury of a large kitchen. This city kitchen gets it all done with an economy of space designed for efficiency of movement. You can reach the sink, stove, and refrigerator from the same spot. One uninterrupted countertop, stretching about 48 in. long, is all you really need.

◀THE OLD ADAGE "small is beautiful" applies here. This modest kitchen incorporates a blurring of the building and furnishings—the same adobe forms the shelves and alcove for the cabinets. Two tall pantries take the place of overhead cabinets. Colorful objects and artifacts and a vintage stove make this kitchen fun as well as functional.

▶ THIS SMALL BUT OPEN kitchen has a casual air to it. Compact kitchen hutches flank a stove that's big enough for serious entertaining. Drop-down cabinet doors serve as countertops or prep areas, and the nearby table is another prep area. A window seat with storage drawers is just outside the kitchen, and additional storage is scattered around the room.

▼ CABINETS DON'T HAVE TO BE continuous around the perimeter of a kitchen to work well. Free-standing units like these are flexible to assemble in a room that is interrupted by odd window configurations. A high-backed bench forms part of the cabinet-work as it shields the side of the island and sets off the kitchen from the dining area.

How Wide? How Tall?

IN THE 1950S, manufacturers of kitchen cabinets standardized the sizes of their products to accompany the new streamlined and modern appliances—range, refrigerator, dishwasher—that were making their way into housewives' kitchens. These standards still remain, although rules are being bent every day:

• Kitchen counters are generally 36 in. high and 24 in. or 25 in. deep.

• Allow at least 12 in. of counter space on either side of a range or cooktop.

• Allow at least 18 in. of counter space next to a refrigerator or oven (for putting down hot or heavy items).

• An overhanging counter needs to be at least 12 in. deep to be useful as a breakfast bar.

• Allow a minimum of 24 in. for each person to stand or pull up a stool at a counter.

• The space between upper and lower cabinets should be a minimum of 18 in.

• An adult needs 30 in. along a table to be comfortable while eating and to avoid knocking elbows.

◄ A SMALL COUNTRY KITCHEN in an older house makes use of limited space with tall, open shelving. The diagonally laid floor tile helps to visually expand the small room, and the center worktable doubles as a breakfast spot.

▼ WHEN THIS SPACE was renovated, a small galley kitchen got a new state-of-the-art range (hidden behind an old exterior) and a granite-topped island. A new dining alcove opened the space dramatically and incorporated storage and two more ovens.

STORAGE

▶LOWER CABINETS and open shelves make for easy access, particularly good for younger and older members of the family, and for often-used items in general. Heavy appliances are also easily accessed when just off the counter. Smoked glass doors keep damaging light and food spatters off the spices, and they are easy to wipe down.

▲THIS KITCHEN doesn't have the traditional parade of upper cabinets—the storage is low and in the island, making it accessible for an older couple or kids. In keeping with the emphasis on easy access, casement windows over a sink are easier to open than double-hung windows.

◀ONE OF THE NEWER trends is having built-in refrigerator drawers integrated into the cabinets. Drawers generally offer easier access than the traditional freezer compartment in a refrigerator, particularly for individuals with mobility limitations.

▲ THERE'S LOTS OF DRAWER and cabinet space in this kitchen, which keeps it from feeling cluttered despite its modest size. Bonus storage is located underneath the corner bench, demonstrating how well-designed storage can make use of otherwise wasted space.

◄ A KITCHEN ISLAND featuring a slant-top bin for bulk items is the centerpiece here, conjuring up images of an old-fashioned general store. The trusses above make a great spot to store a collection of baskets.

Pets in the Kitchen

FAMILY PETS usually spend much of their time getting underfoot in the kitchen, so devote some planning to their needs. Consider where they'll sleep, how they get in and out of the house, where their food and water will be, and where to store their food, toys, leashes, and crates/carriers for traveling.

▲PETS ARE VERY IMPORTANT MEMBERS of the family, and they need their designated spots too. This unique doghouse lets Spot be close to the action but not underfoot, and the lost cabinet space is made up for by the clever bank of storage built along the basement stairs.

▲THIS UPSCALE "STORAGE" SPOT for the family pet is nestled in the cabinetry between chimney flue and dining counter, keeping him out of the way but perfectly poised to clean up any falling scraps.

Dining Areas

Meals are a time to gather the family around the table and recount the highlights (and lowlights) of a busy day. In the past, it was customary to sit at the same table every night, but with the advent of larger homes, we now have several choices of dining spots: stools at a counter; the dining nook; part of a great room that incorporates kitchen, living, and dining space in an open plan; outdoor tables; or even a separate formal dining room.

There are myriad dining-area configurations, and selecting the right one for your family will depend on the layout of your house and your lifestyle. For instance, people who do a lot of dinner-party entertaining for social or business reasons may choose to keep a designated formal dining room, while more casual entertaining may call for a dining space that's connected to, but not part of, the kitchen proper.

▼THIS OPEN SPACE offers three places to eat—at the counter (far right), the dining table (center), and the smaller table at the end of the room, where a woodstove creates a focal point for the seating area. When entertaining a large family group, kids, teens, and adults each get their own table.

▶ WITH A BUILT-IN BENCH on two sides and lots of pillows, this dining area is also a good place for lounging. Abundant storage is built into the benches, making good use of otherwise dead space, and the cabinet at the end of the bench helps define the dining area while lending bonus storage to the room.

▼ IT'S CONVENIENT to have the stairway descend directly into the family center, with its dining area, storage wall, and fireplace. The grid pattern of the stair railing, the support for the countertop, and the storage wall tie the room together.

OPEN DINING AREAS

▲ALFRESCO DINING after dusk is illuminated and warmed by an outdoor fireplace—this could be a place for two to share an intimate dinner or the ideal location for a family wienie roast.

▲IN THIS RECLAMATION of an older building, oversized windows and the exposed structure give the feel of an old schoolhouse, with the couch and bench defining the different activity zones. In the dining area, a view to and from the kitchen makes the space seem larger.

▶PEOPLE IN THE KITCHEN and seating area beyond can both see the dining area, but not each other—the high wall that separates them is thick, creating an alcove on the living-room side for a TV, and a display shelf in the kitchen.

▲THIS SPACE OFFERS CASUAL and formal dining areas, both organized around a fireplace and wood-burning pizza oven. You could have a sandwich at the island or a more organized meal at the dining table. During parties, the countertop holds drinks and hors d'oeuvres, while the main course can be served at the table.

▶IN THIS DINING AREA, there are comfortable couches where the family can stretch out before supper and keep the cook company, as well as plenty of overflow seating if the dining table is fully occupied.

◄ THIS KITCHEN IS VISIBLE but set apart from the dining area by an island and a large cabinet with open shelves on the back side. The exposed framing on the underside of the second floor adds height to the room. The best hosts have extra chairs scattered around for when company drops in.

◄ A DINING ALCOVE has been created by bumping out the wall and further defining the space with the chandelier and window placement. Note the change in the direction of the flooring that distinguishes the dining space from the seating area beyond.

▶ALTHOUGH THEIR SIX CHILDREN are grown and gone, these empty-nesters didn't head for a condo—they wanted to keep their home as a place where the extended family could all get together. The vivid yellow wall, which houses a fireplace in the opening, divides the space into two dining areas. Shown here is a place for informal eating at a custom-made "picnic table."

▼THIS DINING AREA is a few steps down and seems almost to sit in the yard with the table positioned among the grouped casement windows. Whoever's on dish duty can chat with those who linger at the table.

◀AT THIS HOUSE, you get a full dose of morning light with a table located right in the door space. The doors have a multitude of muntins, creating a sort of trellis-like screen between indoors and out. The warmth of the sun is soaked up through the south-facing windows and door (a common and very effective passive solar heating measure).

◄ MIXING THE OLD AND THE NEW can bring the generations together in a family home, and although this house is detailed with traditional materials and moldings, the extra-tall ceiling gives the dining area a very contemporary background for its antique furniture and built-in cupboards. A modern incarnation of the old-fashioned woodstove heats the space efficiently.

◄ THIS ADDITION to a 1912 Arts and Crafts house would make Frank Lloyd Wright proud. The simple yet elegant dining area has plenty of room for extra chairs to be pulled up, and the built-in storage echoes the style of the furniture. The ceiling is as important a surface to consider as any other. Here supporting floor joists above the dining area made it necessary for the decorative box beams below. Many light sources at the ceiling level cast an even glow across the room.

DINNER TABLE ELBOW ROOM

No matter the size or shape of your table, you still need to maneuver around the seated diners. Allowing 24 in. to 30 in. between a table and a wall, and 36 in. to 42 in. between a table and adjacent circulation or living space is optimal. For comfortable seating, allow 30 in. per seat, 24 in. minimum.

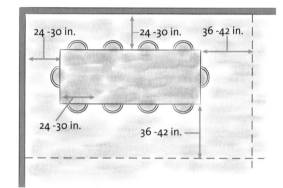

▲ IN THIS UNUSUAL SPACE, the door frame is interrupted by a massive brick chimney, which visually connects the welcoming dining area and the adjacent kitchen beyond. The beehive stove, recessed display niches, and extra-long table with its hodgepodge of chairs work together to create a sense of history and family tradition.

▶ THIS ROUND TABLE puts everyone on equal footing and is a good spot for a game of cards as well as a dining space. The transom windows over the bank of doors are operable, allowing fresh air in when the doors are closed.

FORMAL DINING ROOMS

▲DINING ROOMS don't have to be gloomy, grown-up spaces. This one houses a whimsical collection and a grandfather clock in a room that inspires conversation among young and old alike. A separate dining room should be large enough for the table to take in extra leaves so there's plenty of elbow room at the table.

◀A DINING ROOM that is visually connected to the rest of the house is more likely to be used. Here, the switchback stair pauses at the landing to observe the dining area.

▶ A SEPARATE DINING ROOM is a traditional configuration, but using French doors rather than walls to define the space prevents if from being completely isolated. A view through the room to the windows lends a sense of transparency to the space.

▼ IN THIS HANDSOME Craftsman-style great room, the floor pattern accentuates different zones, setting off the dining area while highlighting the display cabinets. To be versatile and effective, dining room lighting should be dimmable and variable for different occasions.

Family Play Spaces

FAMILY PLAY SPACES ARE FOR THE KID IN ALL OF US, and they can be found throughout the house. These are the places in the home where some or all of the family gets together to play. They may be part of a larger room, or they may be a room dedicated solely to the pursuit of amusement. The most versatile play spaces are capable of growing with the family: A room that initially houses blocks and stuffed animals will eventually need to accommodate video games, darts, or even a pool table.

Durable surfaces that are relatively easy to clean and alter as kids grow will help ensure that a play space serves a family for a lifetime. Regardless of whether the playroom is a converted attic or basement or whether it's a designated corner of the living room, well-planned storage will keep the clutter out of family fun.

▲ IN THIS RUSTIC HOME, the attic was removed to give this game room extra height. The assortment of window types adds to the playfulness of the space, which is perfect for cards or board games—not to mention the pool table—while the exposed beams impart an informal homey feel.

◀ ABUNDANT, ACCESSIBLE storage and plenty of room to stretch out on the floor are two essential ingredients for any play area. Located right off the kitchen, this is the perfect spot to keep little ones occupied but still close enough to supervise. The snack counter is easily accessed through the kitchen window, so Mom or Dad can serve without walking around. In addition to a rugged carpet, there's washable flooring under the easel.

DEDICATED PLAY SPACES

▼THE ULTIMATE IN INDOOR PLAY! If the climate permits only a few months for swimming, then bring the pool indoors, add a spa and a slide, and all the kids in the neighborhood (adults too) will want their birthday parties here! Cedar planking lines the walls and the ceilings, creating a continuous and warming texture throughout the expansive space.

▲THIS UNIQUE LOFT is accessed via a climbing wall, making part of the fun getting to the play space. An interesting curved ceiling follows the roofline, and in another unusual twist, the walls are white, but the ceiling has color. The chalkboard door lets the kids get artistic without getting out a lot of supplies.

◄RAINY DAYS are no problem if there is room inside to set up camp. Attic rooms or rooms over the garage make great playrooms. These spaces can also change over time—today's playroom is tomorrow's hobby room or gym.

▲HERE'S A LARGE SPACE dedicated to one pursuit. In a room of this size and configuration, a high ceiling is more comfortable, and the paneled wainscoting adds warmth. The rack holding the cues, which sits within a shallow niche framed like a doorway, adds an interesting but practical architectural element to the wall.

◀ TEENS WILL HEAD for the family game room instead of the mall with a room like this at home. The floor in this walk-out basement is on grade, so the weight of a heavy pool table is not a problem. Stone floors can be chilly in the winter, so warm things up with rugs.

▼ THIS BASEMENT has the look and feel of a pub, with pool table, deluxe bar complete with wine rack, and even a popcorn machine—it's the ultimate adult play space. A ceramic tile floor is one of many flooring choices that will work over a concrete slab base. It's durable, stylish, and easy to clean, but it's not as kind to bare feet or tumbling glasses as carpet would be.

◄ THE LOW CEILING HEIGHT in this basement, along with the possibility of needing to reach water pipes overhead, dictated that a ceiling system of removable tiles was the best option. In this casual space subdivided into several activity zones—workout, kids' play, and bar—the tiles are both functional and aesthetically suitable to the space, particularly with the inclusion of adequate recessed lighting.

The Converted Basement

A DARK AND DANK basement can be converted into a terrific living or play space. Here are some tips on how to do it:

- Maximize ceiling heights; you want a minimum of 7 ft. to be comfortable. If ceilings are low, recessed lighting works better than hanging fixtures, which eat up even more headroom.

- Because basements tend to be somewhat damp, materials used for floors, walls, and ceilings should repel mildew. A below-ground basement is a potential flood zone in wet weather, so wall-to-wall carpeting is not always a wise selection. Better options for floor materials include vinyl tile, rubber flooring, a floating laminate wood floor (like Pergo®), or even just an area rug tossed over a concrete floor. Walls can be wood paneled or drywall, and options for the ceiling include drywall or a dropped or panelized acoustic ceiling system, which allows access to all the plumbing and electrical lines that inevitably run through a basement.

- Ventilation in warmer weather can be accomplished by an air conditioner if you don't have a walk-out basement. If a window is not available for the air conditioner, a dehumidifier will keep the air from getting musty in the summer.

- Sufficient artificial light from above is more effective than side windows, but windows should always be preserved if you're lucky enough to have them because they dispel that basement feel.

▲ THIS INDOOR BASKETBALL COURT is a far cry from the hoop nailed up on the garage, and it should keep the whole family in shape while ensuring Junior a spot on the varsity team. Wood trusses support the peaked roof of this specialty rec room, and bare stud walls provide nooks and recesses for equipment storage. The space could also be used for indoor volleyball, badminton, soccer, or garage band practice.

▶ THIS CREATIVE PLAY SPACE is a whimsical haven for kids but sophisticated enough for adults to enjoy as well. The room is unified with a graphic theme, from the shelving to the ceiling beams to the checkerboard backdrop behind the "stage." There's even a chessboard painted on the table. To add to the playful aura, wooden replicas of favorite cartoon characters, such as Pink Panther and Roadrunner, hang from the ceiling above the beams.

MULTIPURPOSE PLAY SPACES

◄ WHEN THE OWNERS OF THIS CHICAGO ROW HOUSE needed more space, they converted an adjacent rental apartment into open family space—using part as a nursery for their child and part as a family room.

▼ A ROOM WITHOUT MUCH ARCHITECTURAL CHARACTER needs a layering of furnishings to enliven it, especially if it's to be worthy of a kids' play space. This one uses built-ins, murals, layered rugs, and colorful accoutrements to raise the level of design in a boxy space. There's plenty of room for kids to stretch out and play on the floor, as well as a comfortable seating area for adults.

▲ IN THIS ADULT PLAY SPACE, dropped soffits and encased posts and beams are used to define the three regions of the room: bar, billiard, and seating areas. Glass block in the window opening lets the light in while preserving privacy and is a good option when the view is uninspiring.

▶ EVEN UNEXPECTED SPACES can become a spontaneous playroom, such as this area behind the stairs. It's a space where kids can see and be seen but still have a sense of privacy and freedom. An imaginative railing encases the stairway, suggesting a fort or stage and providing the backdrop for endless imaginative pursuits, while built–in storage under the landing holds lots of toys and saves the larger room from kid clutter.

Family Game Night

FAMILIES ARE SPENDING more time nesting these days, and the idea of getting the family together to play games—board games, cards, chess, or checkers—has made a comeback. All ages can participate, and there's nothing like a heated game of Monopoly to rev up the sibling rivalries and inspire conversation, recounting family lore, or spilling family secrets.

Game night will be more successful if there's a special place for it—something cozy (next to a fireplace would be ideal) with lots of comfortable seating along with a generous table for the game. If you have the space, nothing beats a dedicated game room, but game night can just as easily find a home in the corner of a living room or even around the kitchen table. The real key is making it the place that feels most like home.

▼ FOR VERY YOUNG CHILDREN, basement and attic rec rooms (or playrooms in other remote areas of the house) don't work very well, because the kids want to be near their parents and require a fair amount of supervision. So partitioning off a playroom for the tykes located near the kitchen makes good sense, and it's a great way to effectively utilize a dining room that rarely sees any dinner action.

Home Entertainment

GONE ARE THE DAYS when the television was black and white and the number of channels was limited to thirteen; today a home must accommodate a wide array of electronics: TVs, stereos, VCRs, DVD players, and video and computer games. Some homes are able to devote a separate room to the "media center," which offers the luxury of closing off that space when your teenager and all her friends want to listen to music—loudly. This space might also double as the family computer room or a guest room. In smaller houses, the home entertainment components are often found in the living room.

Cabinetry, acoustics, and wiring are key concerns when designing this space, regardless of where it's located. In some families, the TVs and other gadgetry are deliberately kept behind closed cabinet or closet doors and remain a secondary focal point, while other families enjoy their media equipment out in open view, claiming all the attention. This is a design decision that will influence the furnishing and the arrangement of seating and lighting.

▼ IN THIS HOUSE, the playroom, library, and home theater are all in one room. And although there is no variation in the floor or ceiling planes, the room gets some spatial variety from the bank of built-ins and fireplace that parade down the length of one wall. The large screen and speakers are built right in. The pool table at the other end of the room occupies those who don't like the movie.

◄▲IN THIS ELEGANT MEDIA ROOM, the cabinets are cleverly built in to tuck under the sloped ceiling. The stone chimney breast is capped by a four-paneled wood chimney portion, which gracefully arcs to match the fireplace shape while framing the mantel. When it's show time, the movie screen drops down out of a narrow channel in the ceiling and the video projector pops down from its own concealed space.

◄▼NO MORE WAITING in line at the multiplex—and the popcorn's much cheaper. For avid cinema buffs, it's not hard to put a theater in your own home: just buy some comfy seats and invest in a video projection setup. The brains of the operation and storage for videos and CDs can be concealed in an easily accessible closet.

Acoustics

IN ROOMS THAT HAVE too many parallel hard surfaces, sounds reverberate and make it unpleasant to enjoy music, a movie, or even conversation. Think "texture" and soften up the surfaces by adding carpets, rugs, acoustic ceiling material, and cushy seating; you'll get improved acoustics with a fuller sound and less "bounce." Locating your speakers is a balancing act between woofers and tweeters, and much of it depends on the quality of your equipment.

◄THIS ROOM IS GEARED toward a slightly older crowd, making it the perfect teen hangout with pool table, TV, and Internet access, or a place for the adults to retire after dinner. The massive, built-up ceiling beams lend character while being an effective architectural solution to mask mechanical systems.

Media Center Checklist

WHETHER IT'S IN A FREESTANDING home entertainment center or built-in shelving and cabinets, getting the equipment set up can be frustrating if you haven't thought it through ahead of time. Important considerations include:

- Noise—ideally this area is away from the main living space and has doors and good insulation.
- Access to adequate power outlets and cable hookups.
- Pull-out shelves to reach the back of the equipment.
- Storage for videotapes and DVDs, with room to grow for the stuff that hasn't even been invented yet. Drawers with custom slots for each of these items make it easier to find the one you're looking for.
- The actual audio equipment takes up a few shelves, but your music library also has to be accommodated. Vintage LPs, cassette tapes, and CDs need to be near the audio equipment, and depending on the size of your collection, you might need a separate closet or cabinet nearby to store the music.
- Although most electronic components today don't generate a lot of heat like their predecessors did, you should check the manufacturer's information about how much ventilation space is needed above and behind your components.
- Label the wires when setting up, so if components are moved or rearranged, you're not starting from scratch.
- Speaker locations are best decided while the walls are under construction so that you can pull wires easily. If you're "inheriting" the space, you can use the shelves and outlets that are already there, or adapt the setup to your particular system.

OPTIMAL TV VIEWING

Video technology changes constantly, but family gatherings around the tube haven't changed since "The Ed Sullivan Show." Optimal viewing distances are determined by the size of the TV and the distance and angle of the seating.

W=Width of screen

10 –12 W

A viewing angle greater than 90 degrees begins to make the image look distorted

▲EVERYONE CAN WATCH his or her own program with multiple TVs and headsets in this well-equipped but understated home entertainment room, where gramophones have been wired as speakers. Flat boards on the ceiling divide it into smaller portions that relate to the wall unit at the far end, and the paneling above the window and the door ties the ceiling trim to the wainscoting.

◄ THIS BUILT-IN TELEVISION cabinet becomes an architectural feature, transferring the visual weight of the ceiling beams down to the floor. An oversize ottoman acts as both coffee table and front-row seating for those who like to lounge up close to the screen.

◄ MEDIA CABINETS tend to eat up wall space, so having the luxury of extra height for windows above permits both to share one wall. Remote-control devices can operate the windows so there's no need for a stepladder.

Getaway Places

GETAWAY PLACES ARE OUR SANCTUARIES—the spaces in the house set apart from the communal rooms and demands of family life. These rooms are a few steps away from the active "public" zones of the house, like the kitchen and living room. Some getaway places have doors to shut out the world, some are off the beaten track from the rest of the house, and some are along the way, in nooks and on landings. The obvious retreats are bedrooms and bathrooms, but a getaway place doesn't have to be a whole room. Perhaps it's just a quiet corner of a larger space with a writing desk or a small seating area; the many recesses and odd corners in a home have great potential as places to escape to.

Getaway places are the terrain of relaxation, whether it's curling up in the window seat to read a book on a rainy day, or escaping to the den for quiet conversation, to the hobby room to paint or sew, or to the master suite for a rejuvenating bubble bath. Regardless of what the room is called, with some mindful planning it's easy to create spaces for quiet comfort that help us optimize our precious leisure time.

◄ A WARM AND APPEALING SPACE, this library invites quiet conversation, reading, or simply reflective meditation inspired by the fire. The bookshelves continue across the top of the doorway, creating the sense of a deep portal separating the space from the bustle of the family room, while the walls of books provide acoustic insulation from the noise of the rest of the house.

Dens and Libraries

OFTEN UNDERUSED AND NEGLECTED, dens and libraries can provide the perfect private escape, whether used for traditional activities, such as reading and letter writing, or in a more contemporary capacity—as a computer workstation, for instance. All it takes is a little planning.

You'll want to be removed from the bustle of the kitchen, and furnishings will be dictated by the prime activities in the room. In a library, you need comfortable chairs with both ambient and task lighting (a mix of natural and artificial) nearby. A family library has something for everyone—favorite children's books, classic literature, best-sellers, reference books, art books, and back issues of magazines. Keep in mind that books tend to multiply, so plan for more bookshelves than you think you need.

For a den, consider what activities you want to undertake there. If the room is used primarily for TV-watching, a sofa is a prerequisite for lounging; if it's a workspace, the furnishings need to be practical but attractive and homey, so you don't feel like you're at work all the time.

▲ THOUGH AIRY AND ELEGANT, this library still exudes comfort and warmth. The chandelier creates the perception of a lower canopy over the seating area, balancing the effect of the cathedral ceiling. The fireplace provides a focal point and, along with the rug, coffee table, and facing couches, makes an intimate sub-area in the larger room.

◄ AN ARCHED PORTAL from the adjacent room signals the entry to this welcoming space, which offers several options as a getaway, housing the TV, fireplace, and a library. The ceiling treatment becomes a useful design device— it imitates a higher, coffered (or "tray") ceiling, but there is only an inch or so between each step.

◀THIS LIBRARY is a great example of smart planning: First, the windows at one end let in plenty of natural light, yet the shelves on the adjacent wall are spared direct sun. Second, bookcases with a lot of vertical divisions are kinder to books than long, open shelves, offering more horizontal support and holding the books upright. Finally, several seating areas allow family members to read independently.

BOOKSHELVES FOR EVERY READER

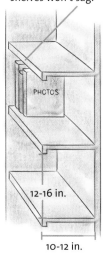

Extra-thick shelf nosing adds reinforcement so shelves won't sag.

PHOTOS

12-16 in.

10-12 in.

FOR HARDCOVER BOOKS AND PHOTO ALBUMS

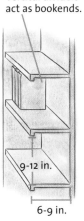

Vertical dividers act as bookends.

9-12 in.

6-9 in.

FOR PAPERBACKS

Tipped shelves let you display books so that kids can find their favorites.

10-14 in.

4-6 in.

FOR OVERSIZED BOOKS AND PICTURE BOOKS

▲WHEN A ROOM HAS several views or focal points, arranging the furnishings is less of a quandary. In this den with three focal points—views to the outside, the fireplace, and the TV—the sight lines were taken into consideration when positioning the seating into groups for conversation. Note that there's plenty of circulation space around the furniture for easy access to the shelves.

WORKSPACE

▲WHETHER IT'S AN OFFICIAL HOME home office or just a place for the family computer, most homes today have some space designated as a work area. This study combines library and computer station, as well as privacy and easy access. The ceiling-height pocket doors can close off the room or be left open so parents can monitor computer use.

▶DON'T OVERLOOK ATTICS and basements when looking for a place to do projects that take up a lot of space—an attic accessed by an out-of-the-way stair will even ensure a modicum of privacy. This handsome space under the eaves has been designated an at-home workspace and is also used as the "editorial and production offices" for a newsletter that chronicles the doings of far-flung relatives.

▲WHEN MORE THAN ONE PERSON uses a study, squabbles for territory are deterred by offering each family member a designated desk area, and in this appealing room, there's one desk for the computer and another for simpler technologies. When trying to open up a small space, painting the ceiling a lighter shade than the walls will visually lift it, as evidenced here where the gray walls stop short of the ceiling by a foot or so, making the ceiling seem much higher.

◀ THE OFFICE OF A work-at-home architect requires considerable storage for oddly shaped items such as models and plans. In this room, positioning the windows above the desktop frees pin-up space below while letting natural light illuminate the work surface. The wall space and quirky nooks and crannies are used to best advantage, and an eclectic assortment of storage options—shelves, cubbies, cabinets—means there's a place for everything. A couch makes it possible to take a break to read to one of the kids.

The Family Computer Checklist

ONE COMPUTER IN A BUSY HOUSEHOLD gets a lot of use, from recording family finances to instant messaging, from writing term papers to gaming, and of course the Internet is a resource that everyone needs. When planning a workspace, consider first who uses the computer and how it is used, which should give you some clues as to where it should be located. Here are some other things to consider when designating a work area:

- Computer space. Unless it's a laptop, you need a surface that's at least 24 in. deep for a computer. It's helpful to have a big enough surface to allow room for files and other papers as well.
- Shelves or desktop space for the printer, scanner, fax machine, and other assorted technology. Remember that you'll have to reach the top, sides, and back of each of these on occasion, so make it easy to access them.
- Electrical outlets with surge protection. These are essential.
- Phone line for modem, if needed.
- Storage for magazines, supplies, stationery, books. Depending on the space available, this could be built-in shelving, cabinets, boxes, or drawer dividers.
- Accessibility. With everyone clamoring for the computer, you'll want to put it in a place where the people using it can get their work done, and in a place where parents can monitor their children's use.

▲AN UNUSUALLY configured space that might be relegated (but wasted) as a catchall storage closet can offer a lot more opportunity with some creative reflection. Here, unusual ceiling framing, low triangular space, and unexpected interior windows combine to create a handsome workspace with built-in desk, counter, and shelving.

▶EVEN A ROOM the size of a walk-in closet can be outfitted smartly as a study if you employ a few tricks to make the best use of the space. This office has a barn-door track that permits the door to slide past the opening for optional privacy. The corner space within has been put to good use for shelving, and the slanting change from wood wall to white ceiling opens up the space.

Nooks

Out-of-the-way spots like window seats, alcoves, and landings make terrific getaway places. If you are designing a new house, don't plan every square inch. Sometimes opportunities reveal themselves during construction that don't appear on two-dimensional architectural drawings—allow for a little serendipitous design.

In rethinking your existing house, look for opportunities for nooks—corners or recesses that can be remodeled or harvested out of eaves, attics, closets, and hallways. A wide hallway can be lined with bookcases or cabinets, and extra-wide or deep landings can host a desk, window seat, or chair. Interior walls thick enough to incorporate alcoves, closets, or bookshelves can also yield a place for a bench or a desk (see illustration p. 101).

▲ IF YOU SAW THIS ROOM on a floor plan, it might be dismissed as inconsequential, but it is actually a total environment, albeit snug. For adults, this getaway conjures up the cabin of a yacht, with its wraparound window seat with a great water view, rich paneling, shiny woodwork, and ladder going to a lookout above. For kids, it's an escape with the feel of an indoor tree house.

◄ USING THE INTERPLAY of geometric shapes in the ceiling and wall planes, the architect carved out an intriguing arrow-shaped nook in the second-story hall space. Exposing the shape of the roof's underside is a dynamic alternative to a flat ceiling, and when lit from above through the large cupola crowning the space, this seating area is a charming spot to relax in.

▶ THE ADDITION OF a post-and-beam wall built 9 ft. out from the existing one-story house helped create a two-story sun space with a dramatic staircase. This is a compelling place for a nap or reading, and magazines and CDs are neatly stored but within easy reach of the built-in seating.

▼ INTERESTING ANGLES created by the sloping ceiling and a snaking, built-in bench intersect to create an intimate spot for cozy late-night reading and TV watching, or a place the kids can hang out during a grown-up party. When planning interior windows like these, take into account acoustics, safety issues, and budget.

▲NOOKS WITHIN A LARGER SPACE create a series of intimate spatial experiences, and part of this second-floor hallway has been transformed into a display area for an antique model boat collection, complete with a custom shelving unit.

◀REMINISCENT OF THE FLOOR lounge in a college dorm, everyone has access to this area overlooking the living room and stairwell, making it a good "sibling neutral" place for watching TV and other leisure activities. Several architectural features define this space, including the two balustrades and interesting ceiling angles, while the rug helps partition off the seating area.

▲ STAIRWAYS AND HALLWAYS wider than the 36-in. minimum required by building code offer great opportunities for desks and storage space. Out of earshot of the family room and kitchen but not totally isolated, this built-in desk is accessible to everyone. The addition of shelves for books and display helps reinvent this landing as a study.

▲ INTERESTING SPACE UNDER THE EAVES yielded this inspiring book nook. The multihued beadboard used for the wall and ceiling creates a striking three-dimensional effect, and the subtle variation in plane enlivens the elevation. The focal point of the space is the unusual bookshelves, with frames built both within and without the end wall.

Carving Out a Small Desk Area

THE MINIMUM WIDTH that will comfortably accommodate a chair and your knees is 24 in. The minimum useful depth for a desk is 18 in. At the very least, you'll want a phone, adequate lighting, and a place for your address book, pen, and paper. If the space is more commodious, you could also include a shelf, maybe even a computer.

Make the space comfortable, taking into consideration desk height (30 in. to 32 in. high), chair height (adjustable is best), the amount of work surface you'll need, and access to storage. Make sure chair or desk corners don't block the normal circulation path in that area.

▼A SIMPLE PLANE defined in space by a sheet of clear glass beckons by its very simplicity. Not much room is needed for a small library and writing desk, and this alcove has a floor-to-ceiling view. With rich mesquite flooring and custom cabinetry, this room within a room is conducive to writing Christmas cards or paying the bills.

▲ADD AN EXTRA 12 in. to a corridor and see how much you can store! Here, a bland interior corridor wall was transformed into a run of bookshelves, with the top shelf reserved for a beloved pottery collection. Stocked bookshelves have good insulation properties, both acoustic and thermal.

FATTENING UP THE WALLS

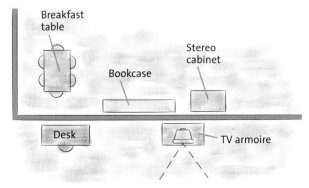

Freestanding furnishings loitering along a long, straight wall do nothing to enhance the architecture.

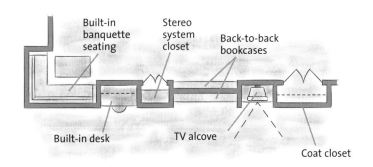

Furnishings can be integrated into the architecture, yielding a more solid-looking wall that is entwined with useful alcoves and closets.

WINDOW SEATS

▲ OFTEN OVERLOOKED, transitional space can be prime real estate. This family took advantage of an extra-wide hallway and its abundant light to incorporate a long window seat that stretches between bedrooms.

▶ A THREE-SIDED BOOK NOOK can also provide extra sleeping space for kids when a capacity crowd comes for the holidays. Leaving the windows curtainless opens the small space and creates the sensation of sitting within the landscape, and when daylight wanes the sconce lighting fixture sheds enough light for reading.

WINDOW SEATS

Depending on whether it is just a perch or an extra bed, a window seat can vary in depth from 18 in. to 30 in. To allow curling up with a good book, deeper is always better.

Light fixture for reading, either at ceiling or mounted on wall or cabinets

Wall or side of cabinet to lean against

Lip keeps cushion from sliding off.

Toe-kick heater or storage below seat

How wide?

Measured from side to side:
• Minimum width for one person to sit is 24 in.
• Two teens tête à tête or one reclining child needs 60 in.
• A napping grownup needs 84 in. to stretch out.

Keep top of cushion below window sill.

▲ SIMPLY BY RAISING the floor up one step and varying the ceiling plane, a whole space-within-a-space is further delineated. Created to serve as a common area in a shared bedroom, this platform window seat/bed annex is the perfect teen hangout for reading, listening to tunes, or even a sleepover.

Spaces for Passions

THESE ARE THE CREATIVE GETAWAYS—the places we go to pursue our favorite interests: music, art, photography, woodworking, and myriad others. We all need some space to indulge our passions and a place to store the stuff that accumulates when we do.

Each pastime dictates specific requirements in a space, but there are some general guidelines. Natural light is beneficial for any activity, especially for art—northern light is ideal because it is soft and stays consistent during the day. Some crafty hobbies require a sink or mechanical ventilation, while others might call for fire-resistant or stain-resistant finish on the floor. Sometimes direct access to the outside is useful—for gardeners or boatbuilders, for example.

These spaces can be flexible—a nursery may be reinvented as an art studio, or a basement toy closet claimed for a darkroom. So remember, when planning these areas consider your particular requirements and plan accordingly for maximum utility.

▲ ONE OF THE MANY advantages of finishing out an attic space is having room to spread out your hobbies. The occupant of this room can work on a sewing project while glancing out the window now and then to keep an eye on the kids.

◄ THIS ART STUDIO housed in a converted garage is outfitted for the whole family, with abundant table room, stools, and storage. Windows at several levels bring in natural light, and track lighting further illuminates the space. Open shelves let you see (and quickly grab) what you've got, but they need to be kept neat or they can look cluttered.

MUSIC

◄ MUSIC IS SHARED by everyone in the family, whether one is listening to it or making it. In this three-level home designed to let the music find its way throughout, the pipe organ is the centerpiece of the ground-floor space.

▼ IN THIS SPACE designed to showcase a beautiful piano, the curved steps and wall mirror the evocative contours of the piano, creating a stagelike setting, and recessed ceiling lights enhance the theatrical effect.

◀ELEGANT FURNISHINGS offset these large instruments, preventing the room from looking like a music showroom or rehearsal hall. Rugs contribute to the balance of the acoustic quality and distinguish the seating/listening area from the performance area. The music area is further divided into two zones by the step up to the harp.

▶PRACTICING MUSIC is a pleasure in this eye-catching getaway, where an Arts and Crafts inspired balustrade, overscale fireplace surround, and unique works of art add visual interest to this creative space. Although this room was placed away from the busiest parts of the house, the double-height space permits musical notes to filter up through the stair landing.

◀▲MOVING THE MUSIC outside to this garage-cum-music studio not only makes great use of otherwise-wasted rafter space (while conserving space within the house, too!), it also ensures that one person's passion won't become another family member's pain. Bear in mind that temperature and humidity can affect instruments and delicate recording equipment. A ceiling fan is used in this space as an inexpensive equalizer—it circulates warm air in the winter, and creates a gentle breeze when it's hot.

ART

▶ EVEN WITH MINIMAL furnishings, this energetic space is filled with places that "occupy" the eye. The intersecting ceiling and roof planes create interest as well as give the impression that the room is larger than it is, while the blank walls become an ever-changing canvas themselves, as the artist adds and subtracts paintings.

▲ HERE, AN ARCHITECT and an artist added a second floor during a renovation, devoting most of it to a work loft. Abundant light is critical for both pursuits, and the windows in the roof let in light from above, while the translucent balustrade maximizes light from the adjacent sun space.

▶ LARGE, OPEN ROOMS invite creativity, and a combination of wall space, natural light, and artificial light are essential ingredients for this art studio. Inexpensive plywood flooring dispels any fear of making a mess, and a mobile supply cabinet grants easy access to paint, brushes, and other tools of the trade.

OTHER PASSIONS

►EVERY CRAFTSMAN NEEDS some designated turf that will be undisturbed by curious hands, but spaces for passions don't need to be large. All you really need is a good work surface, a window, and some storage space, and this inspired spot at the bottom of a spiral staircase fills the bill.

▼WHILE SOME PREFER CLUTTER, others like more austere surroundings to inspire them. The minimal wood trim on the windows and baseboards complements the warm tones of the floor and the hint of pine paneling below, allowing the room to be open, airy, and sunny, and Mom can be creative while the kids read or play. The open stairwell lets the occupants retain a connection to what is happening below.

▶ MAKING HOBBIES a family affair is easy with a long hobby desk like this. It keeps messy projects out of the kids' rooms, and they can share resources like crayons and glue. A hobby desk can also be used for homework, computers, sewing, or laying out the family tree. This deluxe built-in has tons of storage space, two computer stations, and even a concealed laundry chute.

◀ FITNESS IS A PASSION in this house, and having an at-home gym is easier than getting out to the health club when you have young children. A glass block partition separates the exercise area from the relaxation area (sauna and bath), yielding both open and closed zones—a view to the outside from the treadmill and a modicum of privacy for bathers.

►INSTEAD OF DEVOTING A WHOLE ROOM to sewing, the owners made optimum use of an over-sized walk-in closet, installing a "sewing station" amid the usual closet accoutrements.

▲►A CHERISHED COLLECTION—of wine or anything else—demands a well-thought-out location, designed to fit its needs. For wine collectors, basements are the most suitable spot to create a wine cellar because the interior climate can be strictly controlled (see photo above), but any handy little space will do—even a stair landing (see photo at right).

► THIS WHIMSICAL outbuilding is an on-site nursery for a family that's serious about their gardening. The south-facing bank of awning windows, topped by fixed transoms, generates enough warmth to turn the shed into a greenhouse.

▼ IF YOU HAVE A BACK HALLWAY that abuts the kitchen or a bathroom, it's easy to reroute the plumbing and drains to add a sink for the hobbyist. This mudroom has been put to good use for the family gardener, with a sturdy potting bench complete with sink.

Retreats

IT'S IMPORTANT THAT WE TAKE TIME TO RECHARGE from the hectic pace of family life, and our bedrooms and bathrooms are the truly private destinations we head to for quiet, comfort, and self-indulgence. Every family member needs his or her own place for personal pursuits for solitary activities like napping, meditating, or taking a bath.

There are no hard-and-fast rules for creating the perfect retreat. Some people prefer a wide-open bedroom, while others want a personal lair to curl up in. The architecture of the designated space usually suggests one approach or the other, and if there's enough room, a sitting area adds another zone to the bedroom. You can also create a mini-environment within a larger one with a canopy or bunk bed.

A couple of simple solutions can produce a relaxing retreat: a locking door can shut out the world for a time; acoustically insulating the walls muffles outside sounds; and painting the room to your taste helps you personalize the space.

▲▲ A WHIRLPOOL is the perfect place to unwind at home after a stressful day, especially when the candles and wine are nearby. This tub is part of the master suite, but not in the bathroom. If they're willing, parents can share this with the kids.

◀ BEDROOMS THAT ARE DESIGNED to be more than just sleeping chambers offer a retreat that you don't need to be in pajamas to enjoy—this room could be a living room that just happens to have a bed in it. A rug defines the sitting area, breaking the large room into sub-areas, while a picture window frames the view. The fireplace is another focal point, and French doors opening onto a deck extend the footprint of the room outside when the weather is fair.

◄ AN ARC OF CASEMENT WINDOWS frames an alluring sleep area, becoming an elongated headboard. Curved walls present a challenge when furnishing a room; using round tables can help, and putting furniture against a curved wall will prevent you from "reading" the curve in its entirety.

▼ VERY LARGE BEDROOMS can benefit from breaking down the scale of the room into a suite of zones, making it cozier than one big room with a bed at one end. The floor area is broken up into segments by changes in the ceiling plane, and the columns frame the chaise in front of the fireplace. With another chaise near the bed and a window seat next to the bookshelves, this room offers multiple options for relaxation.

ADULT BEDROOMS

◄ THE BEDROOM is the ultimate getaway place—and this one has it all: the luxury of a fireplace, a seating area, a fabulous bed, and doors to the outside to watch the stars on a clear night. The different ceiling heights create an intimate space with the bed placed beneath the lower side; the beams on the high side keep the room from seeming cavernous.

▲ THREE DIFFERENT ACTIVITY ZONES are suggested by the furniture arrangement—a sleep area, a sitting area, and a work area— and each has a grand view of the fireplace and the outdoors. A niche over a fireplace makes an excellent spot to display artwork.

◄ THE FURNITURE does most of the work in this suite as the couch, recliner, and bed define the space, creating different relaxation zones. Because it's hard to hang artwork on sloped walls, the furnishings become the source of decoration.

▲CHANGES IN FLOOR MATERIAL gently define smaller zones within a larger space, and this retreat is geared toward both passive and active pursuits, with assigned corners for sleeping, dressing, and exercising. There's plenty of illumination: The windows in the stairwell rise above the level of the ceiling, suggesting a tower of light in that corner, and the fireplace is raised so that the flames are visible from the level of the bed.

◄THE VIEW AND LIGHT have been used to best advantage by facing the bed toward the window; in quirky or small spaces like this, planning for the position of the bed is critical. A queen-sized bed with flanking night tables needs at least 9 ft. of continuous wall space at its head. Built-in storage drawers take advantage of eave space that might not be used otherwise.

► SUNLIGHT PLAYS OFF the interesting ceiling angles and lovely floors in this bright bedroom. A recess was built to host the TV, VCR, and stereo components, with considerable storage in the cabinets beneath. This inspired treatment is a space-saver and preserves the flow of the rest of the room.

▲▲ A FRENCH DOOR (folded all the way back) closes off this small bedchamber from the sitting area. Adjoining separate spaces like these can have a certain synergy, with one visually "borrowing" space from the other to make a luxurious suite.

◄ BUILDING A BALCONY off a bedroom is a great idea in rural areas, but generally not in the city or suburbs. Here, the contrast in color between the wall and ceiling planes reduces the architecture into simple geometric shapes.

▲CUSTOM-SHAPED WINDOWS are pricey but can make a room special. The rising sun is reflected in the shape of the door opening and in the roof beyond over the balcony. A balcony off the bedroom offers the option of an indoor or outdoor getaway space in the bedroom.

▲THE VIEW'S THE THING in this room, which was designed to catch the mountain scenery from several perspectives, and it even includes doors to the outside for a late-night or early-morning walk in the wild. The overhead truss is silhouetted against the stargazing window at the gable wall, so that even when the curtains are closed you can see the sky.

KIDS' BEDROOMS

▲BUNK BEDS ARE A FAVORITE with kids; when the bed feels like a tree house or the crow's nest on a pirate ship, it adds a playful element to the room. Bunk beds function best when the ceiling is at least 8 ft. high.

▲PAINTED PANELED WAINSCOT can take more abuse than plaster or drywall, and used in a kid's bedroom, it makes a lot of sense. Here, the bay window creates an inviting nook for a dollhouse and other toys, and it allows for a deep sill that adds dimension and interest to the room, as well as a place for display.

▶WITH A CEILING TALL ENOUGH for a tepee, lots of floor space for toys, and all kinds of windows to let the light in, this bedroom makes an ideal play space. Safety is always a concern in kids' bedrooms—don't offer temptation with low windows that have no protection against climbing or leaning out too far. You can limit the extent of a casement or awning's opening.

►BUILT-IN BUNK BEDS with windows and reading lights for top and bottom occupants are ideal because each kid has control of her own light and air flow. This room also sports a terrific amount of storage space, but we know the laws of physics dictate that whatever space is designated for toys will be filled up immediately. Storage used for toys now may hold books, audio equipment, or clothes later on.

▼BUNK BEDS FREE UP space in this small room, and in another space-saving move, comfy floor pillows are used instead of additional chairs. No doubt this rustic retreat is popular for sleepovers because of its camp-like qualities, as the woodsy elements bring the outside in—with a peeled pole and twigwork bunkbed, custom furniture, even a birchbark lampshade.

LOFTS FOR KIDS

A room with a 10-ft. ceiling can hold a loft space if floor space is at a premium.

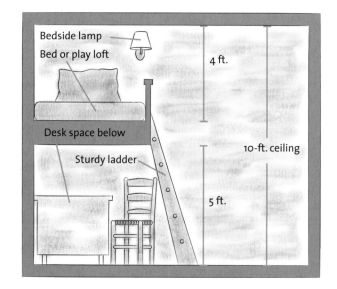

Bedside lamp
Bed or play loft
4 ft.
Desk space below
10-ft. ceiling
Sturdy ladder
5 ft.

▲THE BEST KIDS' BEDROOMS have lots of storage, and both functional and decorative storage abound in this room. In addition to the built-in bookshelf, there's a freestanding one at the end of the bed for the toys du jour. Accessible storage is ideal for kids, because if they can reach it, they might actually use it.

▶A GOOD WAY TO CARVE OUT private alcoves in a shared room is to divide the room by a structural element—in this case a fireplace—giving each occupant her own desk space. This can work equally well in a master bedroom. The dark crown molding adds a pipinglike accent to the room, keeping the walls from blurring into the ceiling.

►THIS ROOM FEATURES a retreat within a retreat. The tall vertical space has three levels: the floor, the window seat, and a loft that is perfect for playing board games or moon-gazing. The area under the loft is intimate, while the ladder reaches up into a more expansive area—the bed is placed to bridge both spaces. When using a ladder as part of the furnishings, remember that sliding access ladders need to be secured to a rail to be safe, and flat rungs are kinder to the feet than round ones.

▲THIS SHARED BEDROOM was designed around an odd-shaped wall with a chimney up the middle, which has been employed to separate the siblings' sleeping areas. Under-cabinet light fixtures are used in a creative fashion for reading in bed, and two rows of display space for books, trophies, and toys assure ample room for both children's possessions. The molding defines the separate and joint space.

Flexible Family Retreats

JUST LIKE the common spaces in a house, getaway places can evolve as the family does, taking on different uses and roles as kids grow up and parents get older.

• For a family with young children, a ground floor playroom with an adjacent bathroom can be useful when kids (and all their friends) are making a mess—at least they won't be tracking it through the whole house. As the children grow up, this same suite can become the master bedroom—peacefully located far away from the teen bedrooms upstairs. It can also become a self-contained guest suite, which any visitor will be thankful for. And finally, it can become an in-law apartment for an aging parent or other relative.

• A very small bedroom can serve first as a nursery, then as a study, and finally a hobby or exercise room when it's time to retire.

• A bedroom's loft can be a playroom when a child is young, a secluded hangout for a teen, and finally a work or storage spot when she goes off to college.

GUEST QUARTERS

▼CUSTOM BUILT-INS that complement the architecture create unique settings that have a longer lifespan because they are traditional, not trendy. In this bedroom, the architecture and furnishings have an old-world Scandinavian style. The refined carving on the decorative archway contrasts with the logs, and the painted wood relieves the natural woodwork. Little conveniences, like a luggage rack and some drawer space, go a long way in making guests feel welcome.

▲PECULIAR OUT-OF-THE-WAY NOOKS and crannies can be put to work as guest quarters or play alcoves, and attics tend to have a lot of these undervalued spaces, which are actually quite charming. Here, a queen-size futon fits perfectly in an alcove with a view and the step up to the bed platform conceals some ductwork.

► HERE'S A PERFECT EXAMPLE of attic space being used wisely. This bright space can be a loft for guests, college kids, or visiting grandchildren—there's room for a crowd here. Tucking the insulation and drywall between massive framing members instead of closing them in adds more life to the space and increases the headroom all around, as does the skylight over the bed.

◄ WITH ITS POST-AND-BEAM construction, whitewashed planked ceiling, and painted beds, this guest room has a Swedish feel. Lighting tucked up at the top of the rafter supports can be left on all night as a nightlight for younger visitors.

►EVERYTHING'S SHIPSHAPE in this yachtlike space where guests are perched over the water. Reading lights are at either side, and the exposed joists overhead are set on an interesting angle, featured against the beadboard inset between them. This would also be a great spot for a slumber party.

◄THIS GUEST ROOM makes maximum use of minimum square footage with built-in storage that creates a window seat and a headboard. A hidden trundle bed provides a great option for overnight guests without taking up additional space. The bedroom door is on a sliding track, yielding even more usable space in the room as you don't have to leave clearance for a swinging door.

BATHROOMS

►SOME TUBS DROP INTO a surrounding deck like this one, allowing the deck and its apron (front) to be custom finished in stone or tile to coordinate with the rest of the bathroom. Separating the tub and shower let the homeowners use wood frames around the windows, which would rot out if they were in a shower space. Shutters over the tub let in the sun but can be adjusted for privacy.

▲SEPARATING THE TUB from the shower takes up a bit more space in a bathroom, but allows for two different uses here: the invigorating wake-up morning shower versus the relaxing soak at the end of the day.

Family Bathroom Checklist

FAMILY BATHROOMS **don't have to be chaotic if they are well planned for** efficiency and safety. Here are a few considerations:

- Separating the toilet from the bathing and sink areas with a partition or door allows for maximum use of the bathroom fixtures.
- Double sinks are a definite advantage for shared bathrooms.
- Kids generally don't start taking showers until they're school age, so be sure there is a tub in the kids' bath. Bathing children can be tough on the back if you're stooping, so plan for enough room to kneel alongside the tub. A spray nozzle in an oversized bathroom sink is good for bathing infants.
- A grab bar in the tub or shower is a must for anyone with disabilities and is handy for everyone else, too.
- Light fixtures over a tub and within a shower have to be watertight and protected with a shatterproof lens according to building codes.
- If there's a whirlpool tub or outdoor hot tub that the kids will be allowed to use, make sure they know how to use it properly. Safety comes first where kids and water are concerned: nonslip flooring around the tub and no large panes of glass nearby.

▲ IN SHARED BATHROOMS LIKE THIS, convenience and privacy issues are key, so two sinks (and two mirrors) are definitely better than one, in either an adult or kids' bathroom. Locating the toilet and tub in an inner, enclosed chamber gives family members access to their sinks while the other fixtures are occupied.

▶TWO TEENAGERS SHARE this well-designed bathroom. Double sinks definitely speed things up on school mornings, and each girl has her own drawers, cabinet, and cubbies for the sizable array of teen toiletries. A skylight in a bathroom is a great idea, letting in extra light but not compromising privacy—and this one can open to bring fresh air into the steamy space.

▲OFTEN, THE BATHROOM is the only room in a family home where you can lock the door and be alone, and this retreat offers several inviting reasons to escape to it. Neutral colors set the tone for relaxation, and multiple wall sconces offer a subtle lighting option at bath time.

▲ INDIVIDUAL CUBBIES can be used for personal toiletries and fresh towels, right next to the shower in a shared bathroom. There are plenty of cabinet manufacturers that offer a variety of bathroom vanities and storage cabinets to match any style.

▲ STORAGE IS PARAMOUNT in a bathroom, and here are two good ideas: the towel storage is in the bathroom rather than the hall linen closet, so no one has to dash furtively into the hall to grab a clean towel; and there's a built-in hamper in the cabinets.

Outdoor Spaces

THE FAMILY HOME doesn't begin and end at the front or back door. A family's favorite pastime may be relaxing in the "outdoor rooms" of the house—the porches, decks, patios, and yards where we can get some fresh air and enjoy the view. These outdoor spaces can be either social places or solitary getaways.

These exterior rooms are the scenes of many family gatherings, from barbecues on the deck to poolside birthday parties to pickup basketball games in the driveway. Our outdoor spaces can also be used for more singular pursuits—an afternoon spent reading in the hammock, planting a new flowerbed, or daydreaming in the tree house.

The most useful outdoor rooms offer a mix of sun and shade, so it's important to take into account the site's natural features (say a large shady tree) as well as the sun's path across the yard during the course of a day. For the most aesthetically pleasing results, consider how best to blend the landscaping (lawn, garden, shrubs) with any hardscape materials (wood, stone) you're considering for an outdoor space, such as a deck or patio.

And finally, don't neglect the transitional spaces—the entryways and mudrooms—that link these exterior rooms with the house's interior. With proper planning, they can be some of the most useful, as well as welcoming, spaces in our homes.

◄ WITH ITS POOL, HOT TUB, tiki bar, and giant deck, this is more than a backyard, it's a family resort! By merging straight lines with undulating forms in this grand space, the combination of natural and manmade surfaces yields an enticing assortment of textures and colors, creating outdoor rooms for different activities. When putting in a pool, plan for whether you want any shade; these saplings look tiny now, but will mature in a few years and cast welcoming shadows on the seating in hot weather.

Transition Spaces

TRANSITION SPACES are the entryways and mudrooms where we move between interior and exterior worlds. Today's busy families aren't seeking the grand foyers of yore—real families need spaces that work hard but still have a sense of style and comfort. These areas need to handle recycling bins, muddy shoes, and high traffic while still being inviting at the end of a long day.

Transition spaces (and particularly back entryways or mudrooms) should be easily reached from the driveway, garage, or street, and their surfaces should be durable—tile, stone, or vinyl—so that they hold up to the daily abuses family life heaps upon them. There are so many durable but attractive options available now that function needn't take precedence over form.

▲ SITUATING THIS MUDROOM a few steps down from the body of the house yields extra ceiling height, freeing up room for cabinets that hold out-of-season items. In this highly organized home, each family member has his or her own space for coats, boots, shoes—even individual baskets for hats and gloves.

◄ OLDER FARMHOUSES always had a mudroom—known as the "back house"—that connected the barn with the kitchen and housed messy tasks, such as canning. This unpretentious mudroom is reminiscent of that time, with all the required attributes—easy access to the outside, storage, a small bench, and durable floor material. Canning jars, gardening tools, drying herbs and flowers, and sports equipment share the space nicely.

▶ THESE RED RUBBER FLOORS are easy to mop and make a good choice in this older house, where they were laid over a slightly uneven subfloor. The narrow hallway is cheered by a large window seat and the oak doors.

▲ IN THIS MUDROOM, all family members get their own locker-like cubbies, making it easy to grab and go. This family prefers gear to be in plain sight, while others may want doors and drawers for a more tidy and formal look.

◄ THE FLOOR AND CEILING materials of this entryway are the same as on the porch, easing the passage from inside to out. The irregular pattern of the stone floor suggests an outdoor patio and also acts as a passive solar collector.

▲A FRENCH DOOR with insulating glass separates the mudroom from the living space and keeps the breeze out on a cold day. A radiator cover under the window offers a toasty seat for pulling on boots (don't obstruct the holes in a radiator cover because they let the heat out). Two rows of hanging hooks ensure that everyone in the family has easy access.

▲ A MUDROOM DOESN'T HAVE TO BE solely utilitarian; this one is used as an appealing display space as well. There can never be enough hooks for hats, and kids are more likely to hang coats on a hook than bother with a hanger. The brick floor is a good choice for a mudroom, but make sure the bricks you select are made for use as a walking surface.

◄NOT ALL HOUSES ARE LUCKY ENOUGH to have tall ceilings like this, allowing for above-closet storage that's perfect for little-used items that are reached by a stepladder. The room's colorful woodwork is shown off to its best advantage against pale walls, and with painted four-panel doors, it takes on a Scandinavian look.

Mudroom Checklist

The ideal mudroom should contain the following:

- A designated cubby for each family member to stow gear
- A bench to sit on. (It should be a minimum of 15 in. deep)
- Hooks for coats and hats
- A place to leave snowy or muddy boots
- A shoe garage for a no-shoes household
- A warm, dry spot for the dog's crate and pet food
- A shelf or hook for leaving keys and pocketbooks
- An emergency kit: flashlight, candles, and battery-run radio
- The dinner bell to call the kids in for supper
- A clock and a mirror for last-minute checks
- An umbrella stand
- As much shelf and cabinet space as can be appropriated
- Seasonal considerations, such as a mitten bin and a beach towel bin

◄ BEHOLD THE ENTRY HALL boiled down to its essence: multiple oversized hooks for speedy hangup, adjacent shelves with baskets for stowing mittens and scarves, and a narrow bench for pulling boots on and off. Staggering upper and lower rows of hooks prevents long items from concealing the hooks beneath them.

► CUSTOM-BUILT CUPBOARDS and cubbies above and below the bench offer abundant storage space in this stylish mudroom. The multipurpose bench is used for pulling off boots or putting down shopping bags, and it has storage for shoes or sports equipment beneath.

▲ THE OWNERS of this colonial-style house wanted to incorporate historic detailing, and the traditional pine flooring in this mudroom is a "living" material that records scratches and scrapes, acquiring a homey patina. Pegs mounted on the chair and picture rails suggest a Shaker-like approach to storing gear.

▶ PLENTY OF FAMILIES shed their shoes upon entry, and this clan has an endless choice of places to put them. A circular bench divided into quadrants serves as a shoe garage, and additional cubbies are in the hallway beyond. Entryways need good light, and this one is lit by the cupola's circular bank of windows.

Porches

LITERALLY SETTING THE STAGE for the rest of the house, the porch is a welcoming area, and it offers a glimpse of the nature of the home within. As a communal space, the family porch is a favorite place for informal gatherings, meals, and entertaining, but it also makes a most inviting retreat for reading or a nap.

A porch has a totally different atmosphere from a deck, offering more shelter and privacy. There are front, side, and back porches, sleeping porches or screened porches, and year-round sun porches. Some have railings that contain, and some have open sides from which you can step out onto the landscape without a care.

A well-planned and thoughtfully furnished porch can help us capitalize on our precious outdoor time. Porches need at least two open sides to catch a pleasant breeze. Unlike a deck that's open to the elements, the porch's overhanging roof protects the finishes and the furnishings. Porches generally have wooden floors, and fir, mahogany, and cedar are the most commonly used materials, though certain porch styles are more conducive to slate or tile flooring.

◄ THE FRONT PORCH is always a welcoming sight (and site) to family members returning home from school, work, or time away, offering a place to perch, shake off the snow, or catch a good-night kiss. The columns at the corners of this porch announce the entrance like two sentries that hold up the porch roof gable above the door. At night, some carefully located illumination is needed, but avoid glaring lights that blind when you climb the front stoop. Light will spill out from the windows as well, so less illumination is better than more.

▶THIS DELIGHTFUL OCEANFRONT porch is perfectly situated for outdoor dining or entertaining. Its groupings of casual furniture relate to each other rather than to the view, enhancing the connection between occupants.

▼A SUNROOM can be used for family events year-round, and this alluring octagonal space can be transformed from a sunroom to a summer porch thanks to an array of double-hung windows outfitted with screens.

THE FRONT PORCH

▲ A PORCH NEED NOT BE LARGE to be functional; 5 or 6 ft. is deep enough to host a bench for taking in the views or just relaxing. The rustic porch was built from boards milled from trees that were on the plot; the tree trunk coming up through the flooring supports it as well.

◄ DURING VERMONT WINTERS, this front porch offers sheltered access to ski equipment, and the open riser stairs leave the stringers exposed to make snow shoveling easy. The porch roof is the primary decorative element of this house's elevation, with the gable's truss and brackets fashioned simply, but elegantly.

PORCH AND COLUMN STYLES

When planning a porch, you'll have a multitude of post and column designs to choose from. Keep the details in the same style as the house to avoid clashing styles. It's a good idea to look at historic examples for proportions. Don't make posts too spindly.

VICTORIAN PORCH STYLE

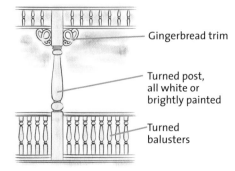

Gingerbread trim

Turned post, all white or brightly painted

Turned balusters

ARTS AND CRAFTS STYLE

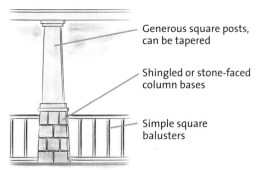

Generous square posts, can be tapered

Shingled or stone-faced column bases

Simple square balusters

CLASSIC COLUMNS

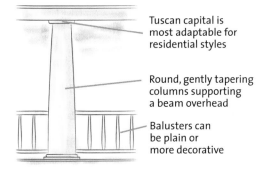

Tuscan capital is most adaptable for residential styles

Round, gently tapering columns supporting a beam overhead

Balusters can be plain or more decorative

▲PAINTING THE FLOORING and underside of the ceiling is a simple, unaffected treatment for this old-fashioned porch that is populated by a family of rocking chairs and a swing. A railing is required only when the porch floor is 30 in. or higher than the surrounding grade, and the solid porch rail here complements the style of the house.

◄▲WHEN A SMALL SEASONAL cottage was remodeled and converted to a year-round residence, the porch was enlarged as well. In the summer, the house now expands to include a charming outdoor dining room that is part of the formal front porch but has the proportion and scale of an interior room. The hipped-roof porch does double duty as an outdoor site for card or board games and puts the porch sitters into the landscape—there's a spectacular garden view and the surrounding foliage provides privacy.

THE BACK PORCH

Porch Surrounds

PORCH SURROUNDS have a dual purpose: to offer protection at the edge of the porch and to decoratively enhance the style of the house. Porch surrounds can be light and lacy, with delicate balusters and a dainty railing under Victorian gingerbread. Porches can also be surrounded by a low partition faced with shingles or clapboard that increase the sense of enclosure.

There are several options:
- Solid or closed balustrade: The surround is built as a half-wall in the same material as the house siding.
- Open balustrade: The balustrade is a series of balusters, vertical elements that run between top and bottom rails, or between top rails and the porch floor.
- Some porches have no balustrade—the porch is not far enough above the ground to require it, or the house predates building code.

▲ WHILE THE FRONT PORCH is on view for the world to see, the back porch is a place to relax in our private domain. This comfortable porch wraps the corner of the house and has several seating areas for those who want to get together or get away. Double-hung windows work well overlooking a porch or deck, and they also make a handy "takeout" area between indoors and out.

◄ THERE'S NOTHING QUITE LIKE rocking on the porch and doing absolutely nothing, and this shallow-depth porch puts you on the edge of the landscape, where you can enjoy a summer rainstorm from underneath a broad, overhanging roof. Peeled tree trunks form the columns that support the ceiling, setting a rustic tone.

▲ A HIGH PORCH CEILING unencumbered by ornamentation mirrors the flat plane of the floor and frames the superior view from this porch. If you're lucky enough to have a view like this, you don't need to do much in the way of design—just let the natural surroundings shine through.

◄ AT THIS SOUTH CAROLINA HOME, outdoor living and dining alfresco are enhanced by a well-appointed porch, where the unusual round columns pay homage to the style of old plantations in the area. This large porch has several zones for a variety of activities.

PORCH NOTES

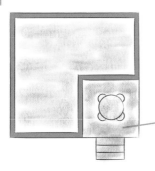

A small corner porch needs only a minimum of 8 ft. x 8 ft. to accommodate a small dining table and chairs for outdoor dining.

In many locales, railings are required only when the porch floor is 30 in. or more above the surrounding grade, but railings offer a pleasant protective feeling surrounding the seating.

Minimum depth 7 ft. to 8 ft. Maximum depth 12 ft. to 14 ft.

ENCLOSED PORCHES AND SUNROOMS

▲ AN OVERHEAD FAN keeps the air moving, making this enclosed porch a cooler alternative to the deck on sweltering days and a splendid spot for a family meal. Be sure the ceiling is tall enough to accommodate a fan like this—if it doesn't hang over a table, the bottom of the fixture needs to be at least 7 ft. 6 in. above the floor.

▶ LITERALLY SEPARATING the public and private zones of the house with an architectural solution such as a breezeway can keep the peace in a family by providing distance between members and offering a neutral spot in between. Here the connecting breezeway between two sections of the house is more than just a shortcut—it's an inspired screened porch that captures every breeze. Custom-made doors and screen panels accommodate the curve.

▲ THIS INFORMAL SCREENED porch gets a lot of nighttime use—surrounded by darkness, the table-top is the center of the universe for a family gathering to play games. Porch lighting is important because at night there's no natural light or reflective pale wall surfaces to cast back some ambient light.

◄ PORCHES ARE TRULY family spaces since they are malleable in function. A porch can be the place where a cherished family collection is displayed, especially if the house proper doesn't offer enough space. This enclosed porch is furnished like a year-round room, complete with rugs and storage.

▼ THE RHYTHM OF THE POSTS around the perimeter of this porch echoes the tree trunks beyond, further blurring the distinction between outside and inside that is created by a screened porch.

▶ TRULY INTEGRATED with its natural surroundings, the family that lives in this captivating space can feel like the Swiss Family Robinson among the trees and rock that emerge from the floor. This garden room is a passive solar collector, and adjacent rooms have windows that open onto it to share the heat and vegetation—especially welcome on sunny winter days in Vermont.

A Porch by Any Other Name...

THE WORD *PORCH* is used loosely to mean any sort of covered way attached to a house. Other monikers include *breezeway, verandah, Florida room, portico,* and of course, *front, side, back,* and even *sleeping porch.* Each has a different connotation tied to climate and culture, but each is inviting and offers a spot to sit.

Then there are the different styles of period porches: Greek Revival, with its distinctive columns; colonial, with simple wooden posts; the elaborately ornamental 19th-century Victorian, Queen Anne, and Gothic Revival porches; and the Arts and Crafts bungalow style. All of these porch styles are being reincarnated by architects today. If you're thinking about adding a porch or remodeling, you'll ensure that you get what you really want by doing your homework and learning the lingo so you can better describe your ideas to an architect or builder.

◀ A SUN PORCH doesn't have to be big to be comfortable. The silhouette of the transom over the French doors is pretty, and the same window arrangement is repeated at the outside walls. At night from outside, the only visual separation between in and out is the lacy pattern of the window muntins, making the room look lanternlike when it is lit up.

▶THERE'S AN ORGANIC FLOW in this house that's achieved in part by French doors in the sunroom opening into a large screened porch beyond, which increases the sense of movement in this home. Paired joists and peeled tree trunks show off the structural framing, giving the architecture an informal tone, and the furnishings follow suit in the form of comfortable beanbag chairs, built-in benches, and rocking chairs.

◀A SCREENED PORCH like this one makes a good place to come in from the sun on a hot day at the beach, or a prime location for the kids to entertain themselves on a rainy afternoon. Screens make an invisible wall and are easily replaced if the crowd gets a little too rambunctious. The matchstick paneling on the ceiling offers a texture and color that sets off the white wicker nicely.

Decks and Patios

Decks and patios expand the footprint of the home to offer a new arena for family fun. If there's an in-ground pool, hot tub, or barbecue area, you're likely to find a deck or patio surrounding it.

Sitting close to the ground but not exactly upon it, decks and patios come in all shapes and sizes, from simple platform decks to expansive multilevel deck-and-patio combinations. The perimeter can take any shape and will be determined by the lay of the land, conforming to the topography by following the natural contours of slopes and plantings.

In addition to the traditional wood and stone building materials, you have the opportunity to incorporate a broad range of ingredients into the mix—water, views, rocks, plantings—when designing a deck or patio. These outdoor spaces need to be equipped and furnished like other rooms of the house, but here the elements are a bit more playful, encompassing umbrellas, grills, built-ins, and fountains, to name a few.

▼GIANT STEPPING STONES made of rainbow pink sandstone from Canada lead the way to this backyard pool. The ground slopes away around the pool, but retaining walls made of irregular cuts of the same stone keep things on the level. Mirroring the design of the owners' Victorian carriage house, the pool cabana provides a place to change, stow gear, and even serve blender drinks at the outdoor counter.

▲EXTRA-LONG BENCHES and lots of uncluttered square footage ensure that this deck gets used often for family gatherings and entertaining. The deck gently inhabits the landscape, making room for several trees to rise up through it, so as not to sacrifice the shade.

◄A WELL-THOUGHT DECK area can establish different activity zones. Here, the gazebo is one destination; it can host a campout or be a refuge from the bugs. Another destination is the deck itself, with built-in benches that offer additional seating for a crowd. The hot tub is used year round, so keep it close to the back door for cold-weather tubbing.

DECKS

▲STURDY RAILINGS are needed for a second-floor deck, and although the building code may require only a 36-in.-high railing, you may want it to be a bit higher when the deck is more than a few feet off the ground like this one.

▶THE TRANSITION FROM built landscape (house) to natural landscape (yard) happens in several stages here, proceeding from the enclosed space of the living room to the open-sided, roofed space of the porch, to the floored space of the deck, and finally to the lawn. The house braces the deck on two sides, so it's not just an afterthought tacked on one end.

Decking Materials

OPEN TO THE effects of the sun and wind, decks need sturdy, long-lasting materials.

The least expensive and one of the most popular options is pressure-treated wood, usually Southern pine, fir, or hemlock. Be aware that the chemicals that make it rot-resistant include a type of arsenic, so if the family dog likes to chew, you may want to reconsider.

Softwoods like cedar and redwood, are beautiful and naturally rot- and decay-resistant, but structurally weaker and more expensive than treated wood. In the South, cypress is another readily available choice in this category.

Then there are the more luxurious tropical hardwoods, like mahogany or ipe, which are durable but expensive, not to mention difficult to work with.

Synthetic wood planking is another alternative, and it comes in several forms: composite materials made with recycled plastics and wood fibers; plastic; and vinyl. Unlike wood, which needs sealant applied every year, the synthetics need virtually no maintenance but are more expensive than wood.

▲THE CASCADING LEVELS of this deck suggest different activities for each, and the pergola overhead also defines the zones and casts some shadows. There's a place for shaded reading or an informal picnic spot at the bench, and sunnier territory for table-and-chair dining sits below.

►SET INTO THE SLOPE of the roof, this small deck is a private nook that makes it possible to have a little solitude outdoors. A second-story deck need not have any stairs to the ground; it can just offer a pocket of fresh air off a master bedroom.

► THIS LUCKY FAMILY can sit
around the campfire at will.
A fire pit draws people together,
and with built-in benches boast-
ing comfortable cushions, along
with festive lights on the underside of the umbrella, this deck is
prime territory for entertaining.

◄ HAVING TREES COME UP through
the decking is a clever touch, as
it gives the sense of being in the
landscape instead of just observ-
ing it. The balustrade has horizontal rungs that may prove tempting
to climb for a child, so this type of
railing is better suited to families
with older kids.

DECK RAILINGS

According to most residential codes, deck railings need to be at least 36 in. high to be safe, and the space between the balusters (the vertical or horizontal pieces) can't be more than 4 in. Railings can be all wood or a combination of materials such as wire, glass, or metal tubing.

WOOD RAILINGS

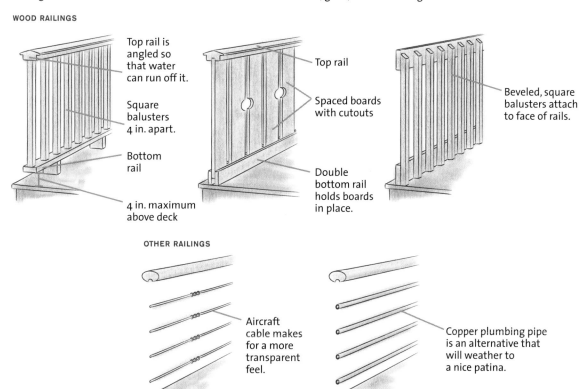

Top rail is angled so that water can run off it.

Square balusters 4 in. apart.

Bottom rail

4 in. maximum above deck

Top rail

Spaced boards with cutouts

Double bottom rail holds boards in place.

Beveled, square balusters attach to face of rails.

OTHER RAILINGS

Aircraft cable makes for a more transparent feel.

Copper plumbing pipe is an alternative that will weather to a nice patina.

◄ A DECK WITHIN THE CROOK of the house is wrapped on two sides by an entry porch and the dining room. Sturdy benches at the perimeter define the edges and offer spots for seating or a plant. Old houses like this traditionally were built low to the ground, so this deck doesn't need a guardrail.

PATIOS

▶SURROUNDED BY LUSH LAND-
SCAPING and defined by stone
walls on several sides, this
dynamic patio continues up
winding steps to another level—
one that is more monolithic looking in the way the pavers fit
together. There is an art to laying
a patio, and the hand of the
artisan is visible here in the way
the naturally shaped paving
stones fit together like a mosaic.
This could be a good project for
an ambitious family to work on
together.

Patio Materials

BRICK, NATURAL STONE, CONCRETE PAVERS, AND POURED CONCRETE
are the primary varieties of patio materials.

• **Brick** is used for walkways and terraces and comes
in a huge range of colors, textures, and shapes, which
can be used in an infinite number of patterns (see the
illustration on the facing page). Vintage brick looks nicely
weathered and blends well with plant materials. It can
be mixed with granite edging or other stone pavers, as
well as wood timbers. With its lumpy surface, brick is not
the ideal material for play areas.

• **Stone** runs the spectrum from natural and rugged
to smooth and refined. Flagstone, fieldstone, and river
rock are popular choices, as are pebbles, which can be
embedded in mortar. You can also buy recut tiles of
slate, granite, and sandstone. Regional materials are
best and will complement the architecture—and they're
often less expensive.

• **Concrete pavers** come in a variety of shapes and
colors. They're easy to use, cheaper than brick, and do
a decent imitation of slate, tile, and brick.

• **Poured concrete** recently has become a versatile
option for patio materials. It can be colored, stained,
sandblasted, or combined with other materials,
yielding many custom options.

►ON THIS COASTAL TERRACE, the surrounding wrought-iron railings have been fashioned into storybook figures that add a whimsical element to what is already a splendid view. Birdwatchers can sit on hand-hewn furniture and enjoy an uninterrupted vista.

▼SITING IS IMPORTANT in all exterior design, and climate and sun angles should inform your choices. The midday sun is too hot to enjoy in some latitudes, so umbrellas or leafy trees are must-haves for poolside dining.

BRICK PATTERNS FOR PATIOS

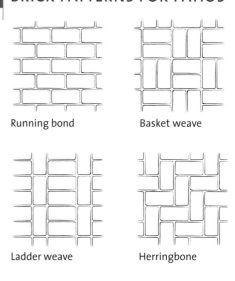

Running bond

Basket weave

Ladder weave

Herringbone

Whorling square

▲ A TIGHTLY SET, random pattern of pavers gives this pool patio the look of a piazza, and the outdoor kitchen (at left) adds another dimension of appeal and usefulness. Before putting in a pool, pay attention to the sun's movements to ensure the pool receives adequate sun, and for family use, safety should be a primary consideration as well.

▶ BEFORE INSTALLING a hot tub, remember that proximity to the house is important, and your patio or deck must be able to withstand the weight of the water and have a nonslip walking surface.

◀ IT'S ALWAYS MORE FUN to host special occasions outside, and an outdoor kitchen is a great advantage (and luxury). It's an old southern climate idea—a "summer kitchen" that doesn't heat up the house in the warm months—and now that notion has been adopted in northern climes as well. This outdoor kitchen has it all—sink, counterspace, dishwasher, even cupboards for the dishes! As with all outside water connections, it's important to make sure there's a frost-free shutoff for the colder months.

▼JUST A FEW STEPS OUT the back door, this spacious multilevel patio area gets a lot of use, from kids' pool parties to adult cookouts. Pools can be cast in lightweight concrete or formed with a vinyl liner, but there is more flexibility for concrete pools to take on unusual shapes, like this one.

Space for Play

EVEN THE NICEST HOUSES can be confining sometimes, and the great outdoors beckons young and old. Whether playing a backyard badminton game, gardening, swimming, or just relaxing in a lawn chair, everyone in the family needs his or her place in the sun.

In planning the yard and play areas, it's important to contemplate whether you want a formal yard or a more natural-looking environment—each requires its own type of planning and maintenance. The formal, manicured yard needs more attention than the more free-form "let it grow" approach. Give every family member a piece of the yard to tend—when they "own" it, there is more pride and enjoyment.

▲ NOT MANY HOMES have a private bocce ball court, so this yard has become a neighborhood gathering spot for some friendly competition. Except for a minor threshold at the door, the patio is at the same level as the indoor space, increasing the apparent connection between the natural landscape and the indoors.

◄ THE DECK OF THIS whimsical tree house envelops the main trunk of an enormous tulip poplar, and the house itself incorporates homey details in its shingled walls and roof that lend a cottage feel. The guardrail is made of store-bought wood lattice mixed with rustic tree limbs.

▼THE BACKYARD doesn't have to have a pool, skateboard course, or fancy toys to be entertaining. This charming outdoor room is formed by two walls sheltered by a tree growing right through the table, and it's the perfect spot for brunch or some quiet reading.

▲THERE'S A PLETHORA of play options for all ages out in this yard: swing set, tetherball (at left), even a sandbox. Setting gravel or wood chips under a swing set will keep it neat and protect the lawn, though it's a little rougher if you take a spill.

▶A COMPELLING VIEW always improves the taste of the meal, especially when you're on the water, and this yard has splendid gardens as well, making it an ideal spot for outdoor dining. A sturdy table under an umbrella is de rigueur for family dining alfresco.

▶ OUTDOOR SPACE is not only for active participation, but also for restful contemplation; this evocative structure, situated at a high point of the garden, provides a sheltered overlook. The lattice adds interest and anchors the seating area.

▼ PART SUMMER HOUSE, part garden shed, this fanciful outbuilding combines storage, a screened porch, and a rainbow roof, making it utilitarian as well as a peaceful destination for play. It's a lovely locale for a lunch break, and the garden tools are accessed from a door at the back.

Fences Make Good Neighbors—and Safe Families

OR YOUNG FAMILIES, nothing beats a secure fence around the play yard. Children have the freedom to run around within its secured borders, without as much parental worry about the street. And fences have the benefit of dissolving any ambiguity about limits—the caution of staying in (or out) of the yard remains pretty clear. And fences offer real protection when it comes to pools and backyard streams. Fencing options include:

- **Split-rail fence.** For any real containment beyond livestock, you'll need to tack wire fence material onto one side.
- **Picket fence.** Traditional wooden pickets can be plain or have decoratively shaped tops. This looks good with almost any style of house and can be bought in premade sections.
- **Stockade fence.** Usually tall and opaque, this is not a friendly option for a front yard, but is good for real privacy out back.
- **Chain-link fence.** This has an urban feel, but is very secure and long lasting.
- **Wrought iron fence.** With a look that's more town than country, this makes a nice background for plantings.
- **Wire fencing.** Cheap and easy to erect, this can be camouflaged by hedges.

◀ BUILT BELOW THE BRANCHES to capture the best views, this waterfront tree house delights visiting grandchildren and also serves as a scenic reading nook for the grandparents. There's easy access via the sturdy stairway, and when you're holed up inside, the corrugated roof material magnifies the raindrops' melody.

► SOME FAMILIES ARE LUCKY enough to have their own waterfront, which opens up all kinds of possibilities for family activities in and on the water. Here, a wooden walkway defines the edge of the lawn and water, and it stretches out the pleasant walk from the house. In planning walkways, remember that two folks walking side by side need about 4 ft. to comfortably stroll.

▲ THE BASKETBALL NET is a fixture in every suburban driveway, and the game is an activity the whole family can enjoy. Here, the foul lines are set in stone pavers, adding some visual interest to this functional and fun space.

Lighting Up the Outdoors

A MOONLIT SUPPER is one thing, but when a teen pool party goes on into the night, outdoor lighting needs to cover a lot of territory.

• Floodlights are harsh and blinding, so try some pole lights with lower wattage bulbs for an even glow, or decorative fixtures mounted on the side of the house or garage.

• Landscape lighting close to ground level adds drama, especially when shrubs and trees are gently illuminated.

• Some fixtures are solar powered and get dimmer as the night wears on.

• Security lights are another story—these can go on automatically by timer or motion.

• Beware of light pollution—too much outdoor light at night can make your yard look like a movie is being filmed there, and it's also unkind to the neighbors and wildlife.

▲COMPLETE WITH LANDSCAPING and a white picket fence, this inspired mini-house can serve many purposes, depending on the age and imagination of the kids using it—fort, castle, hideout, or puppet theater. When the kids grow up, it can be reinvented as a potting shed or mini art studio.

▲▲A SPECIAL VICTORIAN COTTAGE in Lilliputian proportions is a playhouse today but could be a potting shed tomorrow. Before embarking on the construction of outbuildings, check with local officials to determine if you'll need a permit.

▶LOCATE THE SWING SET where it can be seen from the house so a parent can dash out easily in case of accidents. Don't put swing sets too near planting beds, or you increase the risk of trampled plants. Paving stones create a natural terrace designed to allow moss and plants to crop up in between.

SPORTS SPACE

Different outdoor sports require different amounts of space. Standard measurements are given here, but they can be adjusted to fit the space available.

BACKYARD SPORTS

Badminton

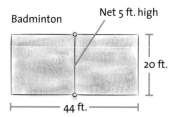

Net 5 ft. high

20 ft.

44 ft.

Volleyball

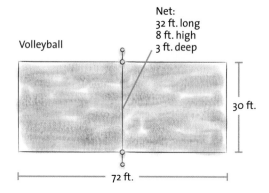

Net:
32 ft. long
8 ft. high
3 ft. deep

30 ft.

72 ft.

Bocce Ball

Width:
13 ft. minimum to
19 ft. 6 in. maximum

Length: 78 ft. minimum to 92-ft. maximum

Croquet

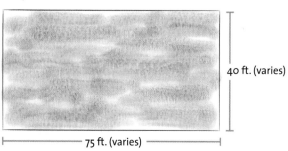

40 ft. (varies)

75 ft. (varies)

DRIVEWAY SPORTS

Hopscotch

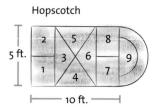

5 ft.

10 ft.

Basketball

4 ft.

15 ft.

Basket on garage wall or freestanding

12 ft.

Four Squares

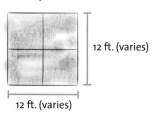

12 ft. (varies)

12 ft. (varies)

▼GENTLY CURVING WALLS and paths imply a destination beyond the trees at this peaceful waterside retreat, where a grassy seating area is framed by stone pavers.

▲THIS LOFTY 80-SQ.-FT. property is a warm-weather retreat for a writer. Rather than rely on the plum tree for structure, it stands on its own posts. For those who work at home, the commute from house to tree house is enough to separate work time from family time.

►THIS COLORFUL PLAY STRUCTURE can be a home away from home for the kids, with its many play zones—ripple slide, swing set, playhouse, and even a swing for adult supervisors. If properly cared for, this can be passed on through the generations. Natural ground covers like cedar chips under a swing set can be easily renewed a few times a year, and they will keep the mud down.

▲OUTDOOR PLAYTHINGS can be temporary, semipermanent, or permanent. This one, made of thick cardboard, can be can be disassembled and recycled at the end of the season. The homemade covered wagon is ready to head to the little house on the prairie, and it has lots of storage nooks for other toys.

Flexible Outdoor Spaces

EVEN THE YARD can change with the family and with the seasons.

- The swing set can make way for a hammock or flower bed when the kids are older.
- An old playhouse can become a potting shed.
- In the winter, you can flood a portion of the yard for a hockey rink.
- The place once occupied by the wading pool might give way to a badminton or bocce ball court.
- In the summer, a birdbath makes a good focal point for the yard; in the winter, make the switch to bird feeders.

▲SHINGLED IN SLATE cut from recycled blackboards, this sauna is a relaxing version of a grown-up tree house. When considering a sauna, keep in mind that it needs a heat source to keep the stones white hot, and a water source to provide the revitalizing humidity, making it potentially hazardous for young family members.

◀ORIGINALLY BUILT as a teahouse for adults, this 300-sq.-ft., multi-level castle in the trees was soon appropriated by the kids. This deluxe tree house took some careful planning: It has electricity, heat, and insulation and is made of local materials with quirky construction. The roofs over the lower portions are curvy and organically shaped, suggesting that tree-dwelling hobbits were at work here.

▲LIKE A TREE HOUSE at ground level, this woodland structure offers a spot to share family lore or tell ghost stories on a dark night. Natural tree trunks make up the columns that support the rustic roof above.

▶IT'S NOT ALWAYS necessary to spend loads of cash or excavate the yard to make a great play area. Here, simplicity carries the day—a piece of plywood nailed to a tree, a homemade ladder, a tire, and piece of rope are all that's needed to create a tree house and swing, offering a desti-nation in the yard when told to go out and play.

Sources

Taunton Press Publications

The Taunton Press publishes many other titles in the Idea Book series on targeted topics or parts of the home, including :

Bouknight, Joanne Kellar. *Taunton's Home Storage Idea Book*. The Taunton Press, 2002.

Bouknight, Joanne Kellar. *Taunton's New Kitchen Idea Book*. The Taunton Press, coming in 2004.

Jordan, Wendy. *The Kidspace Idea Book*. The Taunton Press, 2001.

Wormer, Andrew. *Taunton's New Bathroom Idea Book*. The Taunton Press, coming in 2004.

Zimmerman, Neal. *Taunton's Home Workspace Idea Book*. The Taunton Press, 2002.

The Taunton Press also publishes the following books that are all filled with practical design ideas:

Susanka, Sarah. *The Not So Big House*. The Taunton Press, 1998.

Susanka, Sarah. *Creating the Not So Big House*. The Taunton Press, 2000.

Susanka, Sarah. *Not So Big Solutions for Your Home*. The Taunton Press, 2002.

Tolpin, Jim, with Mary Lathrop. *The New Family Home*. The Taunton Press, 2000.
A tour of 24 homes designed with families in mind.

Fine Homebuilding magazine is also a good resource, especially its special annual issues on *Houses* and *Kitchens and Baths*.

Books

Carley, Rachel. *The Visual Dictionary of American Domestic Architecture*. Owl Books, 1997.
A useful illustrated reference that identifies and describes different styles of architecture (interiors and exteriors), from Federal style to the ranch house.

Hunter, Christine. *Ranches, Rowhouses & Railroad Flats*. WW Norton & Co, 1999.
A good read on the evolution of different forms of American housing, with an emphasis on environmental concerns.

Rybczynski, Witold, *Home: A Short History of an Idea*. Viking Penguin, 1986.
This book has become a classic, discussing the evolution of the idea of home, from medieval times to the present.

Web Sites

www.taunton.com/fhb
The web site of *Fine Homebuilding* magazine has links to a large list of information sites, manufacturers, and publications. Categories include environmentally conscious building, kit homes, kitchen and bath, and tools. This site is also a good source of product and design ideas, and has access to a forum for those interested in home design.

www.build.com
This is a building and home improvement directory that provides links to manufacturers of building products, home products, building publications, and an extensive list of builders, designers, real estate agents, and mortgage brokers.

Professional Organizations

American Institute of Architects (AIA)
1735 New York Avenue NW
Washington, DC 20006
Lists architects who are members of AIA. The website allows you to search for AIA architects in your area.
www.aiaaccess.com

American Society of Interior Designers (ASID)
608 Massachusetts Avenue NE
Washington, DC 20002
Main web site: www.asid.org
For names of ASID members in your area, go to the referral web site: www.interiors.org

American Society of Landscape Architects (ASLA)
636 Eye Street NW
Washington, DC 20001
Web site offers tips on choosing a landscape architect and access to members.
(202) 546-3480
www.asla.org.

Associated Landscape Contractors of America (ALCA)
150 Elden Street, Suite 270
Herndon, VA 20170
Members are a mix of design/build contractors, installation, landscape maintenance, and interior landscape firms.
(800) 395-ALCA
www.alca.org

National Association of Home Builders (NAHB)
1201 Fifteenth Street NW
Washington, DC 20005
Includes builders and remodelers. Website features consumer pages on planning a remodeling project and choosing a contractor.
(800) 368-5242
www.nahb.org

National Association of the Remodeling Industry (NARI)
4900 Seminary Road, #3210
Alexandria, VA 22311
List of contractors.
(800) 611-6274
www.nari.org

National Kitchen & Bath Association
687 Willow Grove Street
Hackettstown, NJ 07840
Members are kitchen and bath design specialists. The web site has projects, remodeling tips, and it lists design guidelines.
www.nkba.com

Credits

CHAPTER 1

pp. 4-5: Photo © Brian VandenBrink, Photographer, 2003, Design: Burt & Weinrich Architects, Damariscotta, ME; p. 5: Photo by Charles Miller © The Taunton Press, Inc.; p. 6–7: Photo © Brian VandenBrink, Photographer, 2003, Design: R. W. Knight Architects, Blue Hill, ME; p. 7: Photo © davidduncanlivingston.com; p. 8: (top) Photo © Mark Samu, Design: Gold Coast Construction, East Hampton, NY; (bottom) Photo © www.bobperron.com, Architect: Charles Marks, Greenwich, CT p. 9: Photo © www.bobperron.com; p 10: Photo © davidduncanlivingston.com p 11: (top) Photo © Brian VandenBrink, Photographer 2003, Architect: Roc Caivano, Bar Harbor, ME.; (bottom left) Photo by Charles Bickford © The Taunton Press, Inc., Architect: Jeremiah Eck, Boston, MA.; (bottom right) Photo by Charles Miller © The Taunton Press, Inc., Architect: Robert Orr, New Haven, CT; p. 12: (top) Photo © www.bobperron.com; (bottom) Photo © 2003 carolynbates.com

CHAPTER 2

p.14: Photo by Tom O'Brien © The Taunton Press, Inc., Builders: Rick Arnold and Mike Guertin, East Greenwich, RI; p 16: Photo © Rob Karosis/www.robkarosis.com, Architect: Dix Shevalier & Associates, Taunton, MA; p 17: Photo © davidduncanlivingston.com; p. 18: (top right) Photo © Brian VandenBrink, Photographer, 2003, Architect: Winton Scott, Portland, ME; (bottom right) Photo © www.bobperron.com, Architect: Robert W. Knight, Blue Hill, ME; (bottom left) Photo © Brian VandenBrink, Photographer, 2003, Architect: Rob Whitten, Portland, ME; p. 19: Photo © Brian VandenBrink, Photographer, 2003, Architect John Morris, Camden, ME; p. 20: (left) Photo © davidduncanlivingston.com; (right) Photo by Charles Miller © The Taunton Press, Inc., Architect: Michael G. Imber, San Antonio, TX; p. 21: Photo © Brian VandenBrink, Photographer, 2003, Architect: Scott Simons, Portland, ME; p. 22: (top right) Photo by Charles Bickford ©The Taunton Press, Inc., Architect: James Stageberg, Stockholm, WI; (bottom right) Photo by Andy Engel ©The Taunton Press, Inc., Architect: Brad Rabinowitz, Burlington, VT; p. 23: Photo © Robert Orr & Assoc. LLC, New Haven, CT; p. 24: (top) Photo by David Ericson © The Taunton Press, Inc., Design: Davitt Design/Build, W.Kingston, RI; (bottom left) Photo by Roe Osborn ©The Taunton Press, Inc., Architect: Todd Hamilton, Dallas, TX; (bottom right) Photo by Leah Babcock-Sherer, © The Taunton Press, Inc., Architect: James Stageberg, Stockholm, WI; p. 25: (left) © The Taunton Press, Inc.; (inset) Photo by Tom O'Brien ©The Taunton Press, Inc., Architects: Brian Reading/William McHenry Architects, Blue Hill, ME; p. 26: (top) Photo © Brian Vanden Brink; (bottom right) Photo © Mark Samu, Design: Langsam Rubin Design, Oyster Bay, NY; p. 27: (top right) Photo © 2003 carolynbates.com; Interior design and general contractor: The Snyder Companies, Essex, VT; (bottom left) Photo © www.carolyn-bates.com, Architect: Ted Montgomery, Indiana Architecture & Design, Charlotte, VT p. 28: (top left) Photo © 2003 carolynbates.com, General contractor: Birdseye Building Company, Richmond, VT; (bottom) Photo © davidduncanlivingston.com; p. 29: (top) Photo © Brian VandenBrink, Photographer, 2003; Architect Winton Scott, Portland, ME; (bottom) Photo © Mark Samu, Design: Lee Najman Design, Port Washington, NY; p. 30: (top) Photo © Ken Gutmaker, (bottom) Photo © davidduncanlivingston.com; p. 31: Photo © Brian VandenBrink, Photographer, 2003; Architect: Burt Weinrich Architects, Damariscotta, ME; p. 32: (top) Photo © Brian VandenBrink, Photographer, 2003, Interior design: Susan Thorn, Cross River, NY; (bottom) Photo © www.carolyn-bates.com, Architect and interior design: Cushman & Beckstrom, Inc., Stowe, VT; p. 33: (top) Photo © davidduncanlivingston.com; (bottom left) Photos © Brian VandenBrink, Photographer, 2003, Architect: Winton Scott, Portland, ME; (bottom right) Photo © carolynbates.com, Designer: Jim Dreisch, Old Hampshire Designs, New London, NH p. 34: (top) Photo © davidduncanlivingston.com; (bottom left) Photo © Brian Vanden Brink; Architect: Van Dam Renner Architects, Portland, ME; p. 35 (top) Photo by Charles Miller © The Taunton Press, Inc.; (bottom left) Photo © davidduncanlivingston.com; (bottom right) Photo © davidduncanlivingston.com; p. 36: (top) Photo © Jessie Walker; (bottom right) Photo © davidduncanlivingston.com; p. 37: Photo © 2003 carolynbates.com, Builder: Erich C. Gutbier, Arlington, VT; p. 38: Photo © Brian VandenBrink, Photographer, 2003, Architect: Ted Wengren, South Freeport, ME; p. 39: (top left) Photo © Brian VandenBrink, Photographer, 2003, Architect: John Martin, Torrington, CT; (top right) Photo © davidduncanlivingston.com; (bottom right) Photo © Brian VandenBrink, Photographer, 2003, Architect: Lo Yi Chan, New York, NY; p. 40: (top right) Photo © Brian VandenBrink, Photographer, 2003, Architect: Mark Hutker & Associates, Vineyard Haven, MA; (bottom left) Photo Charles Miller © The Taunton Press, Inc.; p. 41: (top and bottom) Photo Kevin Ireton, © Taunton Press, Architect: Geoff Prentiss, Seattle, WA; p. 42 (top left) Photo © Brian Vanden Brink; Design: South Mountain Builders, West Tisbury, MA; (top right) Photo © 2003 carolynbates.com, Architect: Brad Rabinowitz, Burlington, VT; (bottom): Photo by Andy Engel © The Taunton Press, Inc.; Architects: Brad Rabinowitz and Don Welch, Burlington, VT; p. 43 (top right) Photo © davidduncanlivingston.com; (bottom left) Photo © Brian VandenBrink, Photographer 2003, Architect: Weston Hewitson Architects, Hingham, MA; p. 44 (top) Photo © Jessie Walker; (bottom) Photo © James Westphalen; p. 45 (bottom left) Photo © davidduncanlivingston.com; (bottom right) Photo © Brian VandenBrink, Photographer 2003, Architect: Lo Yi Chan, New York, NY; p.46 (top left) Photo © davidduncanlivingston.com; (bottom right) Photo © Brian VandenBrink, Photogapher 2003, Architect: Tom Catalano, Boston, MA p. 47 (top) Photo by Charles Miller © The Taunton Press, Inc; Architect: Robert Orr & Assoc. LLC, New Haven, CT; (bottom) Photo by Charles Bickford © The Taunton Press, Inc., Architect: David Sellers, Warren, VT p. 48 (top:) Photo © Jessie Walker, Design: Greene & Proppe Designs, Chicago, IL; (bottom) Photo by Charles Miller © The Taunton Press, Inc.; p. 49 (top) Photo © Jessie Walker, Design: Cynthia Muni, Northfield Ctr., OH; (bottom) Photo © 2003 carolynbates.com, Architect: J. Graham Goldsmith Architects, Burlington, VT; p. 50 (top) Photo by Charles Miller, Design: Bobby Cucullo and Paul Duncker, Wilson, WY; (bottom) Photo © Jessie Walker, Design: Dave Hagerman, Hagerman Kitchens, Lansing, MI; p. 51 (top) Photo © Jessie Walker, Architect: Mastro-Sklar Architects, Chicago, IL; (bottom) Photo by Charles Miller © The Taunton Press, Inc., Designer: Jim Garramone, Evanston, IL; p. 52 (top) Photo © 2003 carolynbates.com, Architect Brad Rabinowitz, Burlington, VT; (bottom left) Photo by Charles Miller, © The Taunton Press, Inc., Architect: Ann Finnerty, Boston, MA; (bottom right) Photo ©Mark Samu, courtesy Hearst Specials; p. 53 (top and bottom) Photos © Jessie Walker; p. 54 (top left) Photo © Mark Samu, Architect James DeLuca, AIA, Huntington, NY; (bottom) Photo by Charles Miller © The Taunton Press, Inc., Designer: Jim Garramone, Evanston, IL; p. 55 (left) Photo © Jessie Walker, Designer: Blair Baby, Wilmette, IL; (right) Photo ©davidduncanlivingston.com; p. 56 Photo © davidduncanlivingston.com; p. 57 (top left) Photo © www.bobperron.com, Architect Paul Bailey, New Haven, CT; (bottom left) Photo © Mark Samu, Builders: John Hummel Construction, East Hampton, NY; (right) Photo © Ken Gutmaker; p. 58 (top) Photo © Mark Samu, courtesy Hearst Specials; (bottom) Photo by Roe Osborn © The Taunton Press, Inc., Architect: Damian Baumhover, San Diego, CA; p. 59 Photo © Jessie Walker; (bottom) Photo © Ken Gutmaker; p. 60 (left) Photo © 2003 carolynbates.com, Designer and general contractor: Dana Ennis, Ennis Construction Inc., Ascutney, VT.; (top right) Photo © Brian VandenBrink, Photographer, 2003; Interior Design: Jane Langmuir Interior Design, Providence, RI; p. 61 (top) Photo © 2003 Rob Karosis/www.robkarosis.com; (bottom) Photo by Tom O'Brien ©The Taunton Press, Inc., p. 62 (top) Photo by Charles Miller ©The Taunton Press, Inc.; (bottom left) Photo © Jessie Walker; (bottom right) Photo © Jessie Walker, Design: Lisa McCauley, McCauley Designs, Barrington, IL p. 63 (left) Photo © Brian VandenBrink, Photographer, 2003, Designer: Tom Hampson, Bluffton, South Carolina; (right) Photo © Ken Gutmaker; p. 64 (left) Photo Charles Miller © The Taunton Press, Inc., Contractor: Christopher Lindsley, Seattle, WA; (right) Photo © Brian VandenBrink, Photographer, 2003; Design Jefferson Riley p. 65 Photo © Brian VandenBrink, Photographer, 2003; Architect: Donham & Sweeney Architects, Boston, MA; p. 66 (top) Photo by Charles Miller ©The Taunton Press, Inc., Architects: Bendrew and Lori Jong, Oakland, CA; (bottom) Photo © davidduncanlivingston.com; p. 67 (top left) Photo © www.carolyn-bates.com, Architect: Malcolm Appleton AIA and Interior design: Barbara Stratton, both of Waitsfield, VT; (top right) Photo by Charles Miller © The Taunton Press, Inc., Architect: Michael G. Imber, San Antonio, TX.; (bottom right) Photo © Mark Samu; p. 68 (top) Photo © Peter Bastianelli-Kerze, Architects: Dale Mulfinger and Steven Buetow, Minneapolis, MN; (bottom) Photo © Mark Samu, courtesy Hearst Specials; p. 69 (top) Photo © 2003 carolynbates.com, General contractor: Roy Dunphy, TreeTop Builders, Inc., Underhill, VT; (bottom) Photo © Ken Gutmaker; p. 70 (top right) Photo © davidduncanlivingston.com; (bottom left) Photo © Jessie Walker; (bottom right) Photo © Brian VandenBrink, Photographer, 2003; Designer: Jane Lang Muir, Providence, RI; p. 71 (top) Photo © 2003 carolynbates.com, Architect: Malcolm Appleton AIA, and Interior design: Barbara Stratton, both of Waitsfield, VT; (bottom) Photo by Charles Bickford,© The Taunton Press, Inc., Architect: Joe Metzler with Skip Liepke; p. 72 (top left) Photo © www.carolyn-bates.com, Architect: Brad Rabinowitz, Burlington, VT; (bottom right) Photo © Mark Samu, Architect: Len Kurkowski AIA, Glen Cove, NY p. 73 (top) Photo © Jessie Walker; (bottom) Photo © 2003 Rob Karosis/www.robkarosis.com; p. 74 (top) Photo © davidduncanlivingston.com; (bottom) Photo by Charles Miller © The Taunton Press, Inc., Architect: Scott Stemper, Seattle, WA; p. 75 (top right) Photo © Carolyn Bates; (bottom left) Photo © Mark Samu; p. 76 (left) Photo © Ken Gutmaker; (right) Photo © Brian VandenBrink, Photographer, 2003, Architect: George Suddell, Westbury, NY; p. 77 (top) Photo © www.bobperron.com, Architect: Burr & McCallum, Williamstown, MA; (bottom right) Photo © Brian VandenBrink, Photographer, 2003, Architect: Bernhard & Priestly Architects, Rockport, ME; p. 78 (top) Photo © www.-bobperron.com, Designer: Diane Yohe, Norwalk, CT; (bottom) Photo © davidduncanlivingston.com; p. 79 Photo © 2003 carolynbates.com, Designer: Donna L. Sheppard, Sheppard Custom Homes, Colchester, VT; p. 80 (top) Photo © Brian VandenBrink, Photographer, 2003; Architect: Centerbrook Architects, Essex, CT; (bottom) Photo © James R. Salomon Photography, Design: Orcutt Associates, Yarmouth, ME; p. 81 (left) Photo ©davidduncanlivingston.com; (right) Photo © Ken Gutmaker; p. 82 (top) Photo © 2003 carolynbates.com, Builder: Erich C. Gutbier, Arlington, VT; (bottom) Photo © James R. Salomon Photography; Design: Orcutt Associates, Yarmouth, ME p. 83 Photo © davidduncanlivingston.com p. 84 Photo © Brian VandenBrink, Photographer, 2003, Builders: Axel Berg Builders, Falmouth, ME;p. 85 (top and bottom) Photos © Brian VandenBrink, Photographer, 2003; Design: Custom Electronics, Falmouth, ME; p. 86 Photos © Brian VandenBrink, Photographer, 2003, Design: Custom Electronics, Falmouth, ME p. 87 Photo © Mark Samu, Design: Langsam Rubin Design, Oyster Bay, NY; p. 88 Photo © www.bobperron.com, Architect: David Goetsch, Stamford CT; p. 89 (top) Photo © Mark Samu, courtesy Hearst Specials; (bottom) Photo © 2003 carolynbates.com, Interior design: Nancy Heaslip

CHAPTER 3

p. 90 Photo © Brian VandenBrink, Photographer, 2003, Architect: Scholz & Barclay Architects, Camden, ME; p. 91 Photo © davidduncanlivingston.com; p. 92 (top) Photo © Brian VandenBrink, Photographer, 2003; Architect: John Martin, Portland, ME; (bottom) Photo © 2003, Rob Karosis www.-robkarosis.com; p. 93 (top) Photo © davidduncanlivingston.com; (bottom) Photo © www.bobperron.com, Architect: Rai Mulbauer, B-L Alliance Architecture, Meriden, CT; p. 94 (top left) Photo © davidduncanlivingston.com; (top right) Photo © Brian VandenBrink, Photographer, 2003; Builders: South Mountain Builders, West Tisbury, MA; (bottom) Photo © 2003 carolynbates.com, Architect: Brad Rabinowitz, Burlington, VT; p. 95 Photo © 2003 carolynbates.com, Architect: Ted Montgomery, Indiana Architecture & Design, Charlotte, VT; p. 96 (top) Photo © Brian VandenBrink, Photographer, 2003; Architect: Winton Scott Architects, Portland, ME; (bottom) Photo © davidduncanlivingston.com; p. 97 (top right) Photo © Robert Perron, Photographer, Architect: Nelson Denny, Hadlyme CT; (bottom left) Photo © Brian VandenBrink, Photographer, 2003; Architect: Jack Silverio, Lincolnville, ME; p. 98 (top) Photo by Roe Osborn © The Taunton Press, Inc., Architect: Bede Van Dyke, Holland, MI; (bottom) Photo ©Brian VandenBrink, Photographer, 2003, Architect: Centerbrook Architects, Essex, CT; p. 99 (top) Photo © Jessie Walker; (bottom) Photo © Brian VandenBrink, Photographer, 2003; Interior design: Io Oakes Interior Design, Boston, MA; p. 100 (left) Photo © www.carolynbates.com, Builder: Jim Converse, Birdseye Building Co., Richmond, VT; (top right) Photo by Roe Osborn ©The Taunton Press, Inc., Architect: Kelly Davis, SALA Architects Inc., Stillwater, MN; p. 101 (left) Photo © Brian VandenBrink, Photographer, 2003, Archi-tect: Stephen Blatt Architects, Portland, ME; (right) Photo by Charles Miller © The Taunton Press, Inc., Architect: Mac White, San Antonio, TX; p. 102 (left) Photo by Charles Bickford © The Taunton Press, Inc., Principal architect: Matt Elliott, Project architect: Bruce Norelius, Blue Hill, ME; (right) Photo © Brian VandenBrink, Photo-grapher, 2003, Architect: Bernhard & Priestly Architects, Rockport, ME; p. 103 Photo © davidduncanlivingston.com; p. 104 (top right) Photo © Robert Perron, Photo-grapher, Designer: Linda Banks, Southport, CT; (bottom) Photo © www.carolynbates.com, Designer: Carol E. S. MacDonald, Colchester, VT; p. 105 (top) Photo by Roe Osborn ©The Taunton Press, Inc., Architect: Kelly Davis, SALA, Stillwater, MN; (bottom) Photo © Robert Perron, Photographer, Architect: Strauss-Edwards Architects, Woodbury, CT; p. 106 (top) Photo © davidduncanlivingston.com; (bottom) Photo by Charles Miller © The Taunton Press, Inc., Architect: John Malick & Associates, Piedmont, CA; p. 107 (left and right) Photos ©2003, Rob Karosis/www.robkarosis.com, Architect: Malcolm MacKenzie, Newton, MA; p. 108 (top left) Photo Roe Osborn © The Taunton Press, Inc., Architect: Bede Van Dyke, Holland, MI; (top right) Photo

© 2003 carolynbates.com, Designer: Carol E. S. MacDonald, Colchester, VT; (bottom right) Photo © 2003 carolynbates.com, Designer/decorator: Robyn Fairclough, Hartland Four Corners, VT; p. 109 (top) Photo © Robert Perron, Photographer, Architect: Lasar Associates, New Milford, CT; (bottom) Photo © Brian VandenBrink, Photographer, 2003; p. 110 (top) Photo © Chris Lovi; (bottom) Photo © Robert Perron, Photographer, Architect: Strauss-Edwards Architects, Woodbury, CT; p. 111 (top right) Photo © Robert Perron, Photographer, Architect: Elena Kalman, Stamford, CT; (left) Photo © Brian VandenBrink, Photographer, 2003, Builder: Axel Berg, Falmouth, ME; (bottom right) © 2003 carolynbates.com, Builder: Erich C. Gutbier, Arlington, VT; p. 112 (top) Photo © 2003, Rob Karosis/www.robkarosis.com; (bottom) Photo © Brian VandenBrink, Photographer, 2003, Architect: Scholz & Barclay Architects, Camden, ME; p. 113 (top right) Photo ©www.carolynbates.com, Designer and general contractor: Ennis Construction, Inc., Ascutney, VT; (bottom) Photo © davidduncanlivingston.com p. 114 (top) Photo © davidduncanliving-ston.com; (bottom) Photo © Brian VandenBrink, Photographer, 2003, Architect: Tom Catalano, Boston, MA; p. 115 (top left and right) Photos © davidduncanlivingston.com; p. 116 (top and bottom) Photo © davidduncanlivingston.com; p. 117 (top, bottom left and bottom right) Photos © davidduncanlivingston.com p. 118 (left and right) Photo © davidduncanlivingston.com; p. 119 (top left) Photo © Brian VandenBrink, Photographer, 2003; (top right) Photo © Brian VandenBrink, Pho-tographer, 2003, Interior design: Drysdale Associates, Washington, DC; (bottom) Photo © Brian VandenBrink, Photographer, 2003, Architect: Theodore & Theodore Architects, Wiscasset, ME; p. 120 (top) Photo by Kevin Ireton © The Taunton Press, Inc., Architect: Cass Calder Smith, San Francisco, CA; (bottom) Photo © Brian VandenBrink, Photographer, 2003, Architect: Peter Bohlin Architects, Philadelphia, PA; p. 121 (top) Photo © Brian VandenBrink, Photographer, 2003, Architect: Weston Hewitson Archi-tects,Hingham, MA; (bottom) Photo © Brian VandenBrink, Photographer, 2003; p. 122 (left) Photo © Robert Perron; (right) Photo © Robert Perron, Architect: Robert W. Knight Architects, Woodbury, CT; p. 123 (left) Photo by Charles Miller © The Taunton Press, Inc., Architect: Keith Moskow, Boston, MA; (right) Photo © Brian VandenBrink, Photographer, 2003; p 124 (top right) Photo © Brian VandenBrink, Photographer, 2003; (bottom left) Photo © Brian VandenBrink, Photographer, 2003, Builders: Rockport Post & Beam, Rockport, ME; p. 125 (top right) Photo © Robet Perron, Photographer, Architect: Nelson Denny, Hadlyme, CT; (bot-tom left) Photo © Brian VandenBrink, Photographer, 2003, Architect: Mark Hutker & Associates, Vineyard Haven, MA; p. 126 (left) Photo © Brian VandenBrink, Photo-grapher, 2003, Interior design: Christina Oliver, Newton, MA.; (right) Photo © Brian VandenBrink, Photographer, 2003, Archi-

tect: Weston Hewitson Architects, Hingham, MA; p. 127 Photo © Brian VandenBrink, Photographer, 2003; Archi-tect: Weston Hewitson Architects, Hingham, MA; p. 128 (left) Photo © Brian VandenBrink, Photographer, 2003; Archi-tect: Weston Hewitson Architects, Hingham, MA; (right) Photo © Brian VandenBrink, Photographer, 2003; Builders: Atlantic Kitchens; p. 129 (left) Photo © Brian VandenBrink, Photographer, 2003, Archi-tect: Weston Hewitson Architects, Hingham, MA; (right) Photo © Brian VandenBrink, Photographer, 2003, Builder: Atlantic Kitchens

CHAPTER 4

p. 130 Photo © Robert Peron, Photographer, Architect: Steve Cavanagh, Hamden, CT p. 131 Photo © Jessie Walker; p. 132 (top right) Photo © James R. Salomon Photo-graphy, Architect: Whitten Associates, Portland, ME; (bottom left) Photo © Brian VandenBrink, Photographer, 2003, Interior design: Jane Langmuir, Providence, RI; p. 133 (left) Photo by Andy Engel © Taunton Press, Inc., Architect: Daryl S. Rantis, Asheville, NC; (top right) Photo © 2003 carolynbates.com; (bottom right) Photo © Brian VandenBrink, Photographer, 2003, Interior design: Christina Oliver, Newton, MA; p. 134 (top left) Photo © Brian VandenBrink, Photogra-pher, 2003; (bottom left) Photo © www.car-olynbates.com, Designer: Pat Pritchett, Vermont Vernacular Design, South Woodbury, VT; (top right) Photo © James R. Salomon Photography, Architect: Salmon Falls Architects, Saco, ME; p. 135 (top) Photo © www.carolynbates.com, Architect: Malcolm Appleton, AIA, Interior design: Barbara Stratton, both from Waitsfield, VT; (bottom) Photo © Jessie Walker, Designer: Dave McFadden, Geneva, IL; p. 136 (left) Photo by David Ericson © The Taunton Press, Inc., Design: Davitt Design/Build, West Kingston, RI.; (right) Photo by Charles Miller © Taunton Press, Inc., Architect: Keith Moskow, Boston, MA; p. 137 Photo © Rob Karosis/www.robkarosis.com; p. 138 (top) Photo © Jessie Walker; (bottom) Photo © Brian VandenBrink, Photographer, 2003, Architect: Centerbrook Architects, Essex, CT p. 139 (top) Photo © Jessie Walker; (bottom) Photo © 2003 carolynbates.com, Builder: Larry Kruse, North Woods Joinery, Jeffersonville, VT; p. 140 Photo © Jessie Walker; p. 141 (left and right) Photos by Charles Miller © The Taunton Press, Inc., Architect: Harry Pharr, Warwick, NY; p. 142 (top) Photo © www.carolynbates.com; (bot-tom) Photo © davidduncanlivingston.com p. 143 (left) Photo © davidduncanliving-ston.com; (right) Photo © 2003 carolynbates.com, Architect: Cushman & Beckstrom, Inc., Stowe, VT; p. 144 (top left) Photo © 2003 carolynbates.com, Architect: Cushman & Beckstrom, Inc., Stowe, VT; (top right) Photo © 2003 carolynbates.com, Interior design: Dee Pomerleau, Burlington, VT; (bottom) Photo © Robert Perron, Photo-grapher; p. 145 (top) Photo © Jessie Walker; (bottom) Photo © 2003 Rob Karosis/www.-robkarosis.com, Builder: Shepherd Builders, Portsmouth, NH; p. 146 (top) Photo

© www.carolynbates.com, Architect: Ted Montgomery, Indiana Architecture & Design, Charlotte, VT; (bottom) Photo © Brian VandenBrink, Photographer, 2003, Architect: Rob Whitten, Portland, ME; p. 147 (top) Photo © Brian VandenBrink, Photo-grapher, 2003, Architect: Peter Bohlin, Philadelphia, PA; (bottom) Photo © Jessie Walker; p. 48 (top) Photo © 2003 carolyn-bates.com, Architect: Malcolm Appleton, AIA, Waitsfield, VT; (bottom) Photo © Mary Gamache Schumer; p. 149 (top) Photo © Brian VandenBrink, Photographer, 2003, Architect: Rob Whitten, Portland, ME; (bot-tom) Photo © Jessie Walker; p. 150 (top) Photo © Rob Karosis/www.robkarosis.com, Builder/developer: The Green Company, Newton, MA; (bottom) Photo © Jessie Walker; p. 151 (top) Photo © Jessie Walker; bottom: Photo © 2003 carolynbates.com; Architect Brad Rabinowitz, Burlington, VT p. 152 (top) Photo © Ken Gutmaker; (bot-tom) Photo © Robert Perron, Photographer, Architect: Robert W. Knight Architects, Blue Hill, ME; p. 153 Photo © Robert Perron, Photographer, Architect: Robert W. Knight Architects, Blue Hill, ME; p. 154 Photo © davidduncanlivingston.com; p. 155 (top) Photo © Brian VandenBrink, Photographer, 2003; (bottom) Photo © Jessie Walker; p. 156 (top) Photo © www.carolynbates.com, Designer: Donna Sheppard, Sheppard Custom Homes, Colchester, VT; (bottom) Photo © 2003 carolynbates.com, Builder: ECG Construction, Arlington, VT; p. 157 (top) Photo © Jessie Walker; (bottom) Photo © 2003 carolynbates.com, Designer: Judy Malachuk, Stowe, VT; p. 158 (top) Photo © davidduncanlivingston.com; (bottom) Photo © Leslie Guerci, Builders: Peter Kahn and James Boughton; p. 159 (top left) Photo © Robert Perron, Photographer; (top right) Photo © Brian VandenBrink, Photographer, 2003, Design: Horiuchi & Solien Landscape Architects; (bottom) Photo © Brian VandenBrink, Photographer, 2003, Design: Weatherend Estate Furniture; Rockland, ME p. 160 (left) Photo by Charles Bickford © The Taunton Press, Inc.; (right) Photo © Korab Photo; p. 161 Photo © Jake Jacob, Treehouse Workshop, Inc., Builder: Treehouse Work-shop of Seattle, WA; p. 162 (left) Photo © Robert Perron, Photographer; (right) Photo © Robert Perron, Photographer, Architect: Felix Drury, New Haven, CT; p. 163 (left) Photo © Robert Perron, Photographer; (top right and bottom right) Photos © Brian VandenBrink, Photographer, 2003; p. 165 (top left) Photo © Jake Jacob, Treehouse Workshop, Inc., Builder: Treehouse Workshop of Seattle, WA; (top right) Photo © Katherine Kamen Landscape Architect, Darien, CT; (bottom) Photo © Rob Karosis/www.robkarosis.com; p. 166 (left) Photo © Brian VandenBrink, Photographer, 2003, Architect: Theodore & Theodore Architects, Wiscasset, ME; (right) Photo by Charles Bickford © The Taunton Press, Inc., Architect: David Sellers, Warren, VT; p. 167 (top left) Photo © Jake Jacob, Treehouse Workshop, Inc., Builder: Treehouse Workshop of Seattle, WA; (top right) Photo © 2003 carolynbates.com; (bottom) Photo © davidduncanlivingston.com